A WILLIAMSON KIDS CAN!® BOOK

The Secret Life of MATH

Discover how (and why) numbers have survived from the cave dwellers to us!

Ann McCallum

Illustrated by Carolyn McIntyre Norton

Williamson Books • Nashville, TN

Library of Congress Cataloging-in-Publication Data
McCallum, Ann.
   The secret life of math: discover how (and why) numbers have survived from the cave dwellers to us / Ann McCallum ; illustrated by Carolyn McIntyre Norton.
         p. cm.—
   (A Williamson's kids can! book)
   Includes bibliographical references and index.
ISBN 0-8249-6779-8 (casebound: alk. paper) — 0-8249-6755-0 (softcover : alk. paper)
   1. Numeration—History—Juvenile literature. 2. Mathematics—History—Juvenile literature. I. Norton, Carolyn McIntyre, ill. II. Title.
   QA141.3.M355 2005
   510'.9—dc22
                                        2005002763

Printed in Italy
10 9 8 7 6 5 4 3 2 1

Kids Can!® series editor: **Susan Williamson**
Interior design: **Carolyn McIntyre Norton**
Illustrations: **Carolyn McIntyre Norton**
Craft styling and photography: **Carolyn McIntyre Norton**
Research: **Carolyn McIntyre Norton, Emily Stetson**
Cover design and cover illustration: **Michael Kline**

Published by Williamson Books
An imprint of Ideals Publications
A division of Guideposts
535 Metroplex Drive, Suite 250
Nashville, Tennessee 37211
800-586-2572

Kids Can!®, *Little Hands*®, *Quick Starts for Kids!*®, *Kaleidoscope Kids*®, and *Tales Alive!*® are registered trademarks of Ideals Publications, a division of Guideposts.

Good Times Books™, *Little Hands Story Corners*™, and *Quick Starts Tips*™ are trademarks of Ideals Publications, a division of Guideposts.

Notice: The information contained in this book is true, complete, and accurate to the best of our knowledge. All recommendations and suggestions are made without any guarantees on the part of the author or Ideals Publications. The author and publisher disclaim all liability incurred in conjunction with the use of this information.

DEDICATION

To Chloe, Chris, and Brent.

ACKNOWLEDGMENTS

I would like to acknowledge
Susan Williamson and Emily Stetson for their untiring efforts
and true talent in the making of this book.
Also, my sincere appreciation goes to Carolyn McIntyre Norton
for her amazing ability to make things beautiful.
Last, a debt of gratitude goes to Ruth and Helmut Klughammer,
who supported me throughout this process and always.

Ann McCallum

DEDICATION

For Daniel, Brian, Caitlin, and Grant.

Carolyn McIntyre Norton

What's Inside

What's the Big Secret, Anyway?

(Yeah, like I really care...)

Okay, that's fair enough. How can you be interested in something that you never really thought about before? For that matter, why would you—or anyone else—care about anything that has to do with math's secret life? Well, maybe, like us, you think that looking back to the beginning of something is a pretty cool thing to do. Or, you just might be a curious kid. If so, then you are one of the lucky people who is about to go on an adventure to discover just how and why math has led such a mysterious and secretive life—and a very, very, very long life at that!

Make that about 35,000 years long! Whoa! So, math has survived longer than languages, longer than ancient civilizations, longer than just about anything that we humans invented

> Yes, definitely, this is more of a detective book than a math book or history book. No question about it.

and discovered. Yes, you can place math and the discovery of fire right at about the same time, historically speaking. And that is even before that most famous invention, the wheel. So, there must be something mighty important about math—or else its long life is just an amazing fluke of history.

If you think about that, you'll come up with some questions that may begin to tickle your curiosity. Maybe you're wondering …

- "Thirty-five thousand years is a long time. How could anything 'survive' that long? And how do you know math has been around that long, anyway?"

- "Who invented math—and why? I didn't even know there were people who could speak that long ago, so how did they begin math? And with all of the things that hadn't been invented, why would math be one of the first?"

- "Did dinosaurs or some other prehistoric animal invent math or stumble across it in some way? Is this some kind of a joke or trick question?"

- "Who kept math alive and who taught it to new generations? And hey—were there schools back then? I thought everyone lived in caves and in huts, trapping animals and looking for shelter."

- "Is this whole book a way to get us to like doing math or is it some kind of way to get us to do math and history homework at the same time? If it is, we're already on to you."

Now, wait a minute. We didn't say that you should be *suspicious* of everything. We said that you might become *curious,* and that is a completely different thing. But to clarify: This book is sort of about math—more as an invention that survived an amazing length of time than about math facts and problems. Because math seems to have "survived" for so long and "traveled" to so many places, it is a lot like history, too.

You were on the right track when you asked about the people, because they play a big role in our detective work, even though they lived so very long ago. Our sleuthing adventure is mostly about discovering and searching for answers. Yes, definitely, this is more of a detective book than a math book or history book. No question about it.

What is a "sleuth" and how do you get to be one?

You have everything you need to be a sleuth with you right now. But to be a Super Sleuth, well, that is something that only you can control. First off, *sleuth* is another word for "detective." And if you are going to be a detective, there is only one kind to be: an excellent one. Otherwise, quite bluntly, why bother?

Here is exactly what you need to be a Super Sleuth:

1. An open mind. That means that you are willing to think about some things that at first glance may seem downright ridiculous to you or at best impossible.

2. Excellent observation skills. In fact, they need to be sharp—even when you are tired. Your five senses will be working overtime. (We didn't say this would be easy.)

3. Curiosity and an adventurous spirit. Without those, you won't get anywhere. But if you keep that mind of yours open to new ideas, curiosity will follow naturally. Trust us on that one.

4. Respect. Respect for what? Why, respect for all of the ideas, beliefs, people, traditions, and ways of doing things that are different from what you know and are accustomed to. Without respect for differences, that open mind of yours will simply slam shut.

That's it. You will want to bring along a small notebook and pencil, just as all good detectives do, but don't stick your head in your notebook when you could be observing and absorbing these experiences firsthand. And for fun, if you have a small camera, bring that along. Ready to move forward—uh, make that move *backward*—in time and place? Great! We're off!

Part I

Keeping Track:

How Humans Invented Methods

Sticks, Stones, Fingers & Bones

So, you're playing the game of Pick-Up Sticks. How do you keep score? *Count the sticks you picked up!* Say you have 2½ weeks until your cousin comes to visit. How do you keep track of the days? *Mark them off on a calendar.* What if your mouth is full of marshmallows, and a friend asks you how many s'mores you've eaten? *You hold up three fingers.*

You get the point. Counting and keeping track—these are things you do every day, many times over. And if you think about it, people from every corner of the globe do these things, too. Actually, as it turns out, people have been using these methods, along with others, for thousands upon thousands of years to answer their

own questions about how many sheep and cows they had, when to plant and when to harvest, and how close by or far away water supplies were. How did they keep track before there was any real concept of numbers? Well, how might *you* have kept track if numbers hadn't been invented yet?

People of long ago, like you, were resourceful. Using what they had available to them—sticks, bones, shells, or clay—all ancient peoples developed systems for keeping track. You'll get a good sense of just how resourceful people were—and how creative they were in their thinking—as we see how different civilizations at different times and in distant lands all came up with systems for keeping track. Whether it was the ancient Greeks and Romans in what is now Europe, using pebbles, balls, and tokens; the people in what is now the continent of Africa using finger counting, or the Inca in South America and the Chinese and Japanese in Asia using knots, ingenuity was alive and well. Other peoples used different objects —pebbles, beans, coconuts, and even dried animal manure—for keeping track.

"It is not once nor twice but times without number that the same ideas make their appearance in the world."

—Aristotle, who lived in ancient Greece, 384 B.C. to 322 B.C.

Any missing?

13

Is that a clue?

In a way. That people used natural materials to help them keep track is a clue to something quite amazing—the resourcefulness of people—but it is not a direct clue to the secret of math's *longevity*, or long life. In detective work, you need to look beyond the obvious to get to the heart of the clues, just as in a good mystery book or on TV detective shows, the puzzle isn't solved until all the clues are put together. Then, the detectives ask questions such as "*Why* did that happen?" or "*How* could they have managed to do that?" Those questions take detectives to the next level of thinking and closer to uncovering the answer.

How will we know what is important?

That is a good question.

Before we get deep into our detective work uncovering the secret to the life of numbers, we should establish the scope of what we are looking at. We all need to begin our adventure with an understanding that we are not looking at the past few decades (10 years), nor at the past few centuries (100 years), nor at even the past few millennia (1,000 years). We are looking back as far as 35,000 years ago … and as recent as yesterday.

Yes, this is a major sleuthing operation that may well cause you to question assumptions that you believe are absolutely true.

And, as each of us knows, that is a very difficult thing to do. For often, it is easier to think more highly of what we know than to do the work of exploring what we don't know. But you're up to the task, aren't you?

Here's a BIG clue to get you started

What is so interesting and so amazing is that *people who lived on different continents and thousands of years apart all developed similar number and counting systems.* How could that be? Those people didn't even know that other humans existed, so they certainly weren't communicating with one another.

What would lead people to develop such similar systems? How could information have been passed along? Or, were these things invented over and over, each time anew? Did numbers have some kind of secret life of their own or were they just a part of the human way of doing things, sort of like walking on two feet?

As we begin, please remember that to be a really good Super Sleuth, you need to keep your mind open to new thoughts, new ideas, and new understanding. Weigh your earlier assumptions against what you read about and think about here. It is only then that you can discover the secrets that are hidden from those who won't entertain new ideas nor seek out answers; it is only then that you may be able to discover the secret to the long life of numbers.

Hatch Marks

How a counting system spanned 35,000 years and several continents

For our first around-the-world (and back-in-time) sleuthing adventure, let's start by looking at an aspect of numbers and keeping track in which we can verify its early use and its use today. This way, we can come to terms with how long ago some of these systems were in place.

To do that, we need to go way back to about 35,000 years ago. Sometime after the discovery of fire but before the invention of the wheel, people began to use bones to make tools and hunting weapons; to make skins into clothes and shelters; to create art on cave walls; and to fashion jewelry out of stones, bones, ivory, shells, and teeth.

And they began to keep track, or count.

They didn't really have numbers, at least not the kinds of numbers that we think of today, but they did have a very simple

40,000 B.C.
Modern humans make tools, art, shelters.

35,000 B.C.
Western Europe: Oldest known notched bones.

30,000 B.C. or earlier
Europe: Earliest known cave paintings.

20,000 B.C.
Africa: Ishango bone with quartz was created.

Quartz

This bone was found in the ancient fishing village of Ishango in what is now the Democratic Republic of the Congo, Africa. It is more than 20,000 years old! The notches are thought to represent a six-month calendar. The quartz was used for making marks.

system that served them well.

These early cave dwellers didn't call it counting or tallying, of course, but the idea was there. People began to *tally* (keep track of) the number of animals hunted or the passage of time by marking notches on bones, or sticks. The oldest examples of these ancient markings have been found on bones in western Europe and Africa.

We call these notched bones *tally sticks.* They are one of the oldest human inventions, along with fire, still in use today.

Today? Yes, we still use tally marks. Have you ever kept track by writing like this? ▚

Tally marks are great for keeping track of items of equal value, such as quarters or dollars you've stashed away or for keeping score in a game. All over the globe, from early humans to today, people have been tallying up!

10,000 B.C.   0   A.D. 10,000

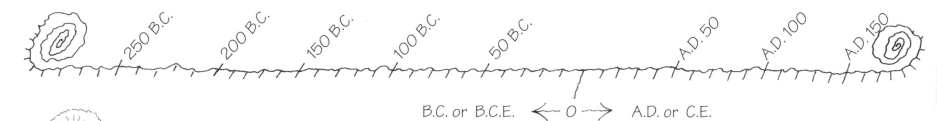

250 B.C. 200 B.C. 150 B.C. 100 B.C. 50 B.C. A.D. 50 A.D. 100 A.D. 150

B.C. or B.C.E. ← 0 → A.D. or C.E.

THINK QUICK!

Figure out this baffling birthday to see if you've got these ABCDE's straight:

How old would someone born in 1990 B.C. be in 2004 B.C.?

Answer to the question is at bottom of page.

TIME TRAVELS

What's all this about B.C.? These letters after the number are a way of marking the modern Western calendar. The people who established our present-day calendar, based on the Christian calendar, divided history into two time periods—the years *before* Christ was born, written as B.C. ("before Christ") and the years *after* his birth, written as A.D. (an abbreviation for the Latin *anno Domini* that means "in the year of our Lord").

Here's the trick: The years in B.C. time start large, way back at the beginning of "modern" human time (40,000 B.C., for instance) and work their way down to more recent time (50 B.C.). The years from Christ's birth forward start with A.D. 1 and increase to the present year.

Many scholars prefer to leave religion out of timekeeping altogether. So you may also see the terms B.C.E., meaning "before the common era," and C.E., for "common era."

Think Quick! answer:
Not old at all! The person wouldn't even be born yet!

Make an Ancient-Styled Tally Stick

TRY THIS!

Since it's not likely many of you need to keep track of animals herded or hunted, you can make a fairly authentic-looking tally stick to keep track of other things. Perhaps you want to mark off every time you manage to save a dollar. Keep track for a few months, or better yet, for a whole year. How much have you managed to save?

You will need:

❖ Cleaned cooked chicken leg bone (remove all meat and wash) or a short stick (with the bark still on)

❖ Penknife (with adult supervision only), or dull butter knife, or fine-pointed marker

What you do:

1 Once the chicken bone has been cleaned, let it air-dry. For those who have permission to use a penknife with the supervision of an adult, use a small branch or twig from a tree or shrub that is about $\frac{1}{4}$" (.5 cm) to $\frac{1}{2}$" (1 cm) in diameter. Shorten it to about 7" (17.5 cm) long. (Leaving the bark on actually helps reveal the markings.)

2 Use the knife or marker to put notches on the bone or stick, similar to the tally sticks found from many thousands of years ago in Europe and Africa.

3 Use it to keep track of your savings or something else like the number of books you've read, or items added to a collection of favorite things!

Tallying in North America

The native peoples in North America also kept track of what was important to them by making tally marks, using feather pens and homemade dyes to make marks on animal hides and tree bark. Do you suppose that they began this practice after learning of it from elsewhere, or do you think that they, too, devised a system that suited their needs?

The three symbols (above) from a Dakota Indian buffalo hide recorded that 30 Dakota Indians were killed in the year A.D. 1800, that food was plentiful in 1845, and that cattle arrived in 1868.

Use Tallies to Take an

 **TRY THIS!** Try keeping count like the American Indians did. Use tally marks to keep track of the wildlife that share your backyard or a nearby park. If you like, take part in the Audubon Society's Christmas Bird Count, too, or other bird counts. Anyone can participate. Just contact the Audubon Society at <www.audubon.org>.

You will need:
❖ Piece of fake suede fabric, or a brown paper grocery bag
❖ Scissors
❖ Markers for the fabric or oil pastels for the paper bag
❖ Piece of string, dried cornhusk, or yarn

American Indian-Styled Nature Count

What you do:

1 Cut a piece of fake suede fabric to look like an animal hide, or cut the bag apart at the sides and smooth it flat. Tear off the edges, giving it a rough shape, like an animal skin.

2 Note the dates you begin and end your count.

3 Design symbols for each kind of wildlife you find and draw them on your paper animal hide. You may want to have a symbol for small birds, one for large ground birds such as wild turkeys and pheasant, another for small critters such as squirrels and chipmunks, and one for larger animals such as deer or fox.

4 Each time you spot a critter, tracks, or other evidence that an animal was nearby, mark a single tally mark line next to its symbol.

5 Store your count by rolling it up and tying it with a piece of string, dried cornhusk, or yarn. Each year, do a new nature count on a new piece of fabric or bag, and compare results year to year. Do you spot any trends? Are you concerned because there are fewer varieties of critters to observe? Are you encouraged by healthy numbers for all types of animals?

KEEP IT SIMPLE: TALLY PROS & CONS

BE A SECRET SUPER SLEUTH

As you track birds and animals, notice how easy it is to use tally marks. You can easily see how many of each type of animal you have observed without using any real numbers. Plus, you can look at the whole "skin" and note what you have seen most frequently and what you've spotted least often. Tally marks are quite an impressive, yet very simple, number system that is as handy today as it was about 35,000 years ago!

On the other hand, when you were saving your spare change (see page 19), you may have noticed one of the problems with tally sticks: Each slash needs to be of equal value. So, if the slash equaled $1.00, did you hold out your spare change until you had a whole dollar or did you jot down the amount with modern numerals until you could make a slash? Either way, without real numbers (which was how tallying was used when it started), it wouldn't have worked for partial amounts. It really was meant for equal whole amounts, as was used on early tally markings. That is not a problem with tallying, of course, but more a limitation as to how it could be used most effectively. Does that tell you anything about the kind of counting skills that were needed when tallies first developed?

Double Tally Sticks

As tallies were used over thousands and thousands of years, new needs actually *did* improve on the original idea. Take a single tally stick. Notch it and then split it in two to keep track of transactions. What do you get? The invention of the *double tally stick!*

The lender kept one half of the stick and the borrower kept the other. Later, when the debt was being repaid, the sticks were compared to check the amount. There was virtually no way to cheat, because the two sides of the tally stick had to fit together and match exactly. So no one could change the amount owed by substituting another stick, as the notches wouldn't match up. Imagine that—tally sticks keeping people honest!

This drawing of an early double tally stick from the Middle Ages in England illustrates how the double tally was made and used.

TRY THIS! Break off a few green twigs from a shrub. Split one in half (horizontally or vertically), and notice the break marks. Set both pieces aside. Now repeat with a second twig, but this time try to match a piece of the first twig with a piece of the second. Do they fit perfectly, or are there indications that this is not a real match?

Tallies & Taxes in Old England

In about A.D. 1100, people living in England used double tally sticks to keep track of taxes, fines, rents, and other money owed.

The founders of the Bank of England also used double tally sticks at this time. When money was put into the bank, the amount

The double tally stick is a perfect example of the secret life of numbers.

As you track numbers' routes from 35,000 years ago, remember the development of the double tally stick. It's an important clue.

These carved tally stocks belonged to an English exchequer in A.D. 1440.

was carved with tally marks onto the double tally stick. The stick was then split in two; the piece retained by the bank was called the *foil*, and the piece kept by the lender was called the *stock*. (One meaning of the word stock is "stick" or "log of wood.") The person with the stock was the *stockholder* and owned a little piece of the bank until he was paid back. Aha! Do you see where this is headed now? If you are thinking of the *stock market*, where people buy and sell ownership in parts of companies (i.e., buy and sell *stock*), then you are right! And to think it all began with hatch marks, about 35,000 years ago.

Finally, in 1826, bank authorities decided to turn to a newer method of record keeping. In 1834, the massive collection of tally sticks stored in the House of Parliament was burned. Unfortunately, the fire got out of control and ended up burning down the entire House of Parliament. Those tally sticks really went out with a roar!

I'M A STOCKHOLDER!

FAST-FORWARD

Today, many countries have a financial center where stocks are traded. There, investors can lend money to different companies by buying stocks, or shares, from the company. Investors then own a little piece of that company until they sell their stocks. The main stock market of the United States is the New York Stock Exchange, located on Wall Street in New York City.

On the trading floor of the exchange, brokers buy and sell securities (stocks). The computer age has completely taken over the exchange now, but the transactions are still all about numbers!

MAKE IT REAL! If you ever visit New York City in the United States, be sure to include a fun visit to Wall Street in your plans. That is where the impressive New York Stock Exchange building is located. While you're down on Wall Street, go to the South Street seaport for a great lunch and to see the sights!

Photo used with permission of the New York Stock Exchange, Inc.

Keep It Fair with Double Tally Sticks

TRY THIS!

Have you ever borrowed money from a family member or promised to do some chores in exchange for a special favor? How did you keep track of what was owed? To keep from being foiled ("fooled") the next time you owe someone money or chores, make your own double tally sticks. Give the stock to the person who lent you the money or favor (the stockholder), and you keep the foil for your own records.

If you wanted to buy a loaf of bread in 17th century England, you'd need to bring your half of a baker's tally like these historic ones.

Bakers tallies.

©Science Museum /Science and Society Picture Library/London

The baker would notch his and your tally sticks at the same time to record your purchases. At the end of the week when you wanted to pay your bill, the sticks were compared to see that the notches matched. You couldn't erase any marks and the baker couldn't add any, so there was never any question as to the amount owed. An ancient wooden credit card!

You will need:

❖ Newspaper
❖ 2 sticks about
½" (1 cm) in diameter and
about 7" (17.5 cm) long
❖ Penknife* (with adult
supervision only)

What you do:

1 Lay down newspaper to protect your working surface. Place the sticks side by side and use the knife, if permitted, to make large, clear tally marks *across both sticks* to represent the amount of the loan. (You may need to come up with a system for showing dollars and cents. For instance, you could use thick lines for dollars and thinner lines for cents.

2 Give one stick to the person you borrowed money from, and put your stick in a safe place. When it is payback time, match the sticks to double-check the correct amount of the money owed.

*No penknife or adult present? Use markers, but remove the bark first.

A VISIT TO THE EXCHEQUER IN THE MIDDLE AGES

MAKE IT REAL

Let's take a time-capsule trip back in time to England in the 12th century. We're just now entering a big, drafty hall in the king's palace where a number of officials are seated at a table covered in a checkered cloth. It's very quiet, as any speaking is done in hushed tones. This department in the king's court is called "The Exchequer" (x-CHE-kar), and as we glance at the checkered tablecloth, we realize that it wasn't randomly selected for our visit. The cloth is part of a calculating device! (But, more on that later ... see page 110.) These officials are in charge of the king's treasury, and they are busy calculating the amount of taxes the king should receive from each corner of the kingdom. Tea is served, which is a good thing, because the drafts in the room are making us all shiver!

One of the officials carves a flat piece of wood with several notches representing the amount of money owed to the king by one of the outer provinces. The size of the notch, we're told, indicates the amount of money owed. For instance, a wide cut about the width of a hand represents 1,000 pounds sterling. (In American dollars today, this is about $1,600, although this number changes each day based on the current exchange rate.) A cut the thickness of a thumb represents 100 pounds, and a cut

> If the stick pieces
> don't match exactly,
> the sheriff will be ...
> let's just say
> he will be in big trouble!

the width of a little finger indicates 20 pounds. (So, that's how they did it! It's not very accurate, but it *is* an improvement over the ancient tally marks.)

The tally stick is given to a clerk who carefully breaks it into two pieces so that the notches extend over both pieces. At that moment, a sheriff who will be responsible for collecting the taxes enters the room. The sheriff is given one side of the broken double tally stick. He will return with this half of the stick as well as the cash when the taxes are due. He knows that the double tally sticks not only help him collect the proper amounts from the people, but they also guard against dishonest sheriffs. At collection time, the two pieces of the tally stick will be put back together, and if the stick pieces don't match exactly, the sheriff will be ... let's just say he will be in big trouble! No wonder that—along with it being cold—we notice a distinct sense of tension in the hall.

One of the officials reminds the sheriff that the king may not want to wait until tax time to get his money. If so, the king's exchequer may sell the king's side of the tally stick to someone else for a discounted price. Then, the sheriff will have to pay this new person when tax time comes along. Either way, the sheriff better fulfill his end of the bargain! For us, well, we're just glad that we don't have to pay any taxes to this sheriff; he looks as if he is all about business!

From then to now and there to here!

So, in the space of a few pages, we have revisited a system of number-like markings and ways to keep track that began about 35,000 years ago and that we still use today. And it was a system that probably began in the areas where the Middle East and Africa are and then eventually traveled to England and North America. Plus, it all began long before different peoples even knew of one another's existence, let alone traveled and spoke to each other.

Turn the page to see how the secret life of numbers managed to keep going in other ways over thousands of years and thousands of miles, too.

Head, Knuckles, Knees & Toes:

"Digit" counting in ancient times

What's your earliest memory of numbers and counting? What are your family members' and friends' first memories of numbers? Are there lots of similarities in the answers you get? Yes, we all did it and most of us still do! Most of us began keeping track of the important things in life—like our ages and how many cookies we ate—by holding up our fingers! After all, our fingers are always with us, and anyone can understand what we mean—no language barriers with finger counting, right?

But if you think counting on your fingers is something new, well, by now you realize that numbers and keeping track go way, way back. Finger counting was probably used by those same

40,000 B.C.　　　　　30,000 B.C.　　　　　20,000 B.C.

cave dwellers who drew hatch marks on cave walls.

When people began counting larger and larger amounts, patterns for counting numbers on fingers began to appear. By adding the use of knuckles, joints, and bones of the hand, people could count much higher. (The Chinese even figured out how to count to 100,000 with one hand and to one million if they used both hands.) In New Guinea, people counted using their whole bodies!

Based on a language thousands of years old, the Kewa people of Papua New Guinea use their word for "hand" to mean "five." In North America, the Takelma people, who lived for thousands of years in what is now southwestern Oregon, used the word *ixdil*, meaning "hands," to mean "ten." In South Africa, the Zulu people have used a system of finger counting since the development of their need for accurate number communication. Fingers and toes: These handy *digits* are the original counting machines—and they are not about to go out of style!

10,000 B.C.

2500 B.C.   0
(North Africa) Egypt:
Earliest concrete evidence
of finger counting.

A.D. 10,000

"BUT, EVERYONE COUNTS WITH THEIR FINGERS!"

BE A SECRET SUPER SLEUTH

Well, here we are—and there we were—people the world over using fingers and toes to count. And even with the ability of the Chinese and others to do some very fancy finger figuring, this practical system of counting was used mostly when there was no need for extremely large numbers. So, Super Sleuth, do you suppose that using fingers or toes—in groups of ten—had anything to do with how our modern-day counting system was developed?

Could the idea of grouping by tens have been "planted" as long as 35,000 or more years ago? Hmmm …

Egyptians finger counting, as depicted here from a monument made about 2500 B.C.

Eenie, Meenie, Minie, Morra!

TRY THIS!

Play Morra, the simple and very popular finger-counting game that's been enjoyed by people the world over throughout time. Even though it is an ancient game, it is still played in Italy, France, Spain, Portugal, Morocco, Greece, Egypt, Syria, Iraq, and China. It's also a good way to choose someone to be "It" for other games!

To play: Two players stand face to face, each holding out a closed fist. On the count of three ("one, two, three!"), each player shows as many fingers as he chooses and at the same time calls out a number from 1 to 10. (If you use both hands, you call a number from 1 to 20.) If the number called by a player is the same as the number of *all* the fingers shown by *both* players, then that player wins a point. Play a certain number of rounds, or play to a certain point score.

P.S. If no one is winning, then either narrow the choices by using only one hand each, or play that the person wins who comes the closest without going higher than the real number.

One, Two, Three... Nye, Bili, Thathu?

TRY THIS!

Learn how the Zulu count by placing your palms face up with all fingers, including the thumbs, bent inward, then follow the pictures below. A Zulu usually says the word for the number as she shows the sign. Notice anything interesting about the meanings for the Zulu words?

  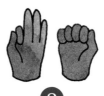  

1
nye
(NAY)
"state of being alone"

2
bili
(BEE-lee)
"raise a separate finger"

3
thathu
(TAH-too)
"to take"

4
ne
(neh)
"to join"

5
hlanu
(THAH-new)
(all the fingers) "united"

6
isithupa
(ee-see-TOO-pa)
"take the
(right) thumb"

7
isikhombisa
(ee-see-com-BEE-sa)
"point with the forefinger
of (right) hand"

8
isishagalombili
(ee-see-shi-a-ga-lom-BEE-lee)
"leave out
two fingers"

9
isishiyagalunye
(ee-see-sha-ga-lo-LOO-nay)
"leave out
one finger"

10
ishumi
(ee-shu-MEE)
"cause to stand"

Finger Counting, Zulu-Style

Within the country of South Africa today lies an area known as Zululand. This beautiful homeland of the Zulu people is also home to many exotic animals, such as elephants, lions, and zebras, as well as fantastic birds and butterflies. Each hut in a traditional Zulu village typically has a woven roof placed on top of a round base structure made from branches and sticks. Inside the hut, the floor is a lovely polished green produced by a mixture of tightly compacted anthill sand (without the ants!) and cow manure (imagine that!). Of course, the Zulu people have been influenced by modern things, but this is how they traditionally live.

In the Zulu marketplace, many people today still use a sophisticated system of finger counting, based on the original Zulu method of counting. A specific finger gesture equals a particular number, and even when the people are gesturing very, very quickly, they manage to understand one another quite well.

> In the Zulu marketplace, many people today still use a sophisticated system of finger counting, based on the original Zulu method of counting.

TRY THIS!

Play Zulu Says

Once you've practiced your Zulu number gestures, see how quickly you can form each one! Gather some friends together to play a game of Zulu Says. Using the same rules as Simon Says but with the gestures for the Zulu numbers, have the leader call out "Zulu says" followed by a number. (You can begin by saying the number in English, but then once you get better at it, use the Zulu word.) The rest of the group forms the number. If the leader doesn't begin by saying "Zulu says," the participants shouldn't respond. If you do, you are out of the game.

Learn American Sign Language! For another version of Zulu Says, use these American Sign Language number gestures!

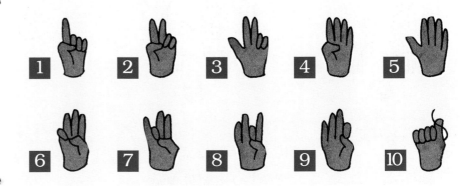

1 2 3 4 5
6 7 8 9 10

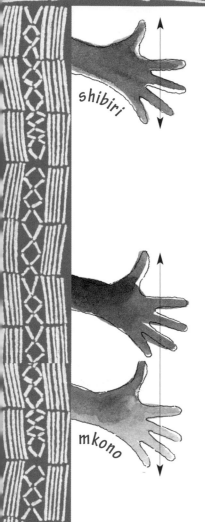

A Swahili Way to Measure—Body-Style

Farther up the African coast, the African Swahili people also used to rely on body-part math, but in this case it was to measure length, rather than to count.

Having an approximate measure worked fine when someone was making one thing at a time, but this system could cause problems in the marketplace. For example, the customer with the longest hand span would get the best deal when buying some cloth. Or, looking at it another way, the seller with the shortest hand span would make the largest profit. Knowing your hand span now, imagine when you would have wished you had bigger hands and when small hands would have suited you just fine, thank you!

A shibiri *was the distance from the tip of the pinkie finger to the tip of the thumb in a spread hand.*

The mkono *was two of these hand spans.*

The pima *was four mkono, or eight hand spans.*

THINK QUICK!

How many shibiri was a pima?

Answer to the question is up the side of this page.

We're off to meet the *quipucamayoc!*

You know, the *quipucamayoc*, or "quipu-maker." Realizing that finger counting in Zulu is a skill far beyond anything most of us have ever managed, we thought you would thoroughly enjoy another skill you may believe you have mastered already—tying knots. Of course, these aren't just any knots tied any which way or in any place. With math and its many secrets, placement, or shall we say, *place value*, are very important. So if you are feeling adventurous and if you are trying to put all of this together to figure out the secret to math's longevity, join us as we head to Peru! (Or, would you prefer China, where knots were used at a much earlier time?)

Would You Like a Receipt? Knot!

How knots & numbers go together

Knots and math?
Uh—this is getting really weird!

Are you one of those people who is good at tying knots? You know—able to tie a bowline, a double fisherman's knot, or a taut-line hitch without a second thought (and without looking it up!). Or, are you more like some of us who have always found tying knots to be somewhat of a mystery? Tying shoelaces is one thing, but knowing the knots that will hold a kayak onto the roof of a car, well, that is something else entirely. And surely, none of us ever really considered our knot-tying skills as having much to

2000 B.C.   1500 B.C.   1000 B.C.   500 B.C.
(Asia) China:
Recording numbers on knotted strings mentioned in I Ching.

In the Inca empire
knots were
the preferred method
of keeping track.

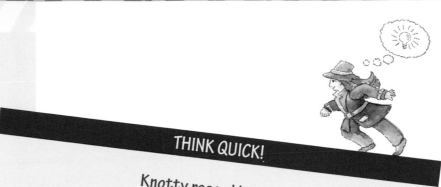

THINK QUICK!

Knotty record keeping

There are earlier mentions of knots and numbers, too. In 500 B.C. in China, knots used in record keeping were mentioned in the *I Ching*, an ancient Chinese book about the basic ideas of everyday life. It is also called the *Book of Changes*. The idea of tying a knot to represent a number has also been found in the Middle East, Nigeria, Hawaii, Japan, and many American Indian cultures, from ancient to recent times.

What is a common memory aid used by many people today that is somewhat similar to the knotted string custom?

Answer to the question is up the side of this page.

do with our number skills, right?

Uh-uh. Sorry to disappoint you, but knots and numbers go together, or at least they went together long ago, especially if you lived in the Inca empire in western South America (about where Peru is today) along about A.D. 1200 to A.D. 1500. There, knots were the preferred method of keeping track.

0   A.D. 500   A.D. 1000   A.D. 1200   A.D. 1500   A.D. 2000

(South America) Peru:
Quipus used
for record keeping.

Why Knots?

A story of what might have happened

Picture this: You are a very wealthy emperor whose land stretches far and wide into the mountains of western South America. It's A.D. 1475 and it is time to collect taxes from those who live on and work the lands. But how do you keep track of who owes what?

(That part is true. The emperor at that time, who lived in the capital city of Cuzco, ruled an enormous expanse of rugged land. And, this family of royals was very wealthy, thanks to the taxes they collected from all the citizens of their empire, called Tahuantinsuyu [TA-wan-tin-suyu], or "The Land of the Four Quarters." There was an incredible system of roads linking all parts of this prosperous empire, and there were even engineered bridges to cross the deep ravines.)

Tracking taxes is the same issue that was solved in earlier times by using tally sticks and by finger counting. We'll learn that the ancient civilization in Mesopotamia, in an area of the Middle East today, at first used pebbles for keeping track (page 60). Pebbles may have proved difficult for the tax collectors of the Inca empire to carry, especially across rugged terrain. The Mesopotamian ancients later used clay tablets with notations on them, but those, we imagine, would have been breakable … and heavy. So, what could they do instead?

The Inca people raised many llamas, and they certainly knew how to weave the wool into yarn. Hmmm … use what is naturally plentiful, right?

So, how did the Inca keep track of everyone's taxes so efficiently? They didn't have a system of notation or symbols for numbers yet. The Inca people invented their own method of record keeping—something permanent, and more important, something easy to carry along the long roads leading to and from the capital. The Inca invented a system of knotted strings!

This amazing quipu was made by an Inca in A.D. 1400- A.D.1532. It is attached to a carved wooden stick.
©Bildarchiv Preussischer Kulturbesitz/Art Resource, NY
Ethnologisches Museum, Staatliche Museen zu Berlin, Berlin, Germany

Instant Messaging—Knot!

Even if there were a system of knots, how to get the message from here to there was the next obstacle. We're talking about a huge empire. And keep in mind the lack of transportation, or anything technological such as phones, e-mails, and the like. How did the Inca overcome that hurdle?

Not to worry, as it wasn't a problem for the Incas! They developed a system of trained runners, called *chasquis* (CHA-skis), to carry information from one place to another. These speedy runners ran as fast as they could between station houses, passing their message on to the next runner, much like a baton is passed on in a relay race. In this giant relay race, a series of runners could cover about 300 miles (480 km) in 24 hours!

How did the runners remember the messages they had to deliver after such a long run? Each runner carried a *quipu* (KEE-pooh), a special record-keeping device that was made out of knotted string. When rolled up, each quipu looked sort of like a mop full of knots, but it was actually a sophisticated way to record amounts such as taxes owed or collected, or how much metal had been taken from one of the Inca mines. Each Inca town, village, and district had a *quipucamayoc*, or "quipu maker," who was in charge of creating and then interpreting the meaning of the knotted strings. String is light and runners are swift. A system of runners in relay was brilliant. Are you impressed by how inventive humans are?

"I THOUGHT OF IT FIRST!"

BE A SECRET SUPER SLEUTH

The Japanese people had a similar system using knotted string called the *ketsujo* (ke-TWO-joe). And Darius, King of Persia (522 B.C. to 468 B.C.), used knotted string, not in the sophisticated way that the quipu was used, but nonetheless it was related to keeping track and using string. Darius is said to have tied 60 knots in a leather strap. He ordered the soldiers, whom he left behind to defend an important bridge, to untie one knot each day. If he didn't return by the time the last knot was untied, all of the soldiers were instructed to return to their homes.

Now, how clever was that!

These diverse examples illustrate that similar devices used for keeping track of amounts appeared in areas far away in time and space. How could these ideas have spread from one civilization to another? Or, maybe they didn't spread at all. Maybe each civilization developed its own system without knowledge of the others. That begs the question: Do you think that humankind is so alike that different people developed similar methods without ever knowing about one another? We think this is very curious and exciting to think about.

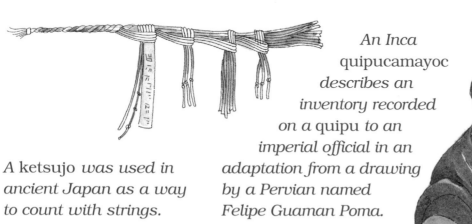

A ketsujo was used in ancient Japan as a way to count with strings.

An Inca quipucamayoc describes an inventory recorded on a quipu to an imperial official in an adaptation from a drawing by a Pervian named Felipe Guaman Poma.

A Closer Look at Quipus

A quipu was a means of recording information. It provided a system for keeping track. These knotted strings were a sophisticated way to document such things as the population, taxes, or amount of livestock or crops. A quipu could be very simple with just a few cords. Or, it could have up to 2,000 cords tied together!

Here's how a quipu worked:

The main, or top, cord had the summation cord and pendant cords tied onto it. The cords could be different colors to represent different items.

Numbers were recorded by using knots in various positions on the quipu. Their placement on the string referred to a power of ten, like 10, 100, or 1,000. The number of knots represented the digits from 1 to 9.

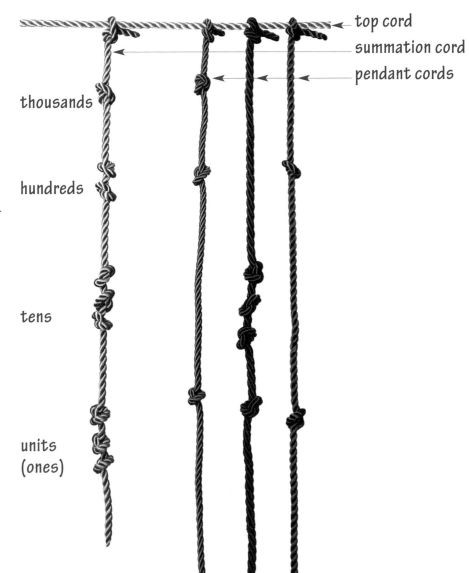

top cord

summation cord

pendant cords

thousands

hundreds

tens

units (ones)

Make an Inca Quipu

TRY THIS!

Here's a "knotty" bit of fun. Let's say it's your birthday and three relatives have given you money: $35 from your aunt and uncle, $20 from your grandma, and $46 from your parents (they included $16 allowance they owed you for the past month). Wow! That's more than you can earn mowing lawns for your neighbors.

So, how can you keep track of how much everyone gave you so that you can write thank-you cards? And, how can you keep track of how much you have altogether so that you can figure out if you have enough for a new computer game or a CD player? Keep track like the people of the Inca empire and make a usable Inca quipu!

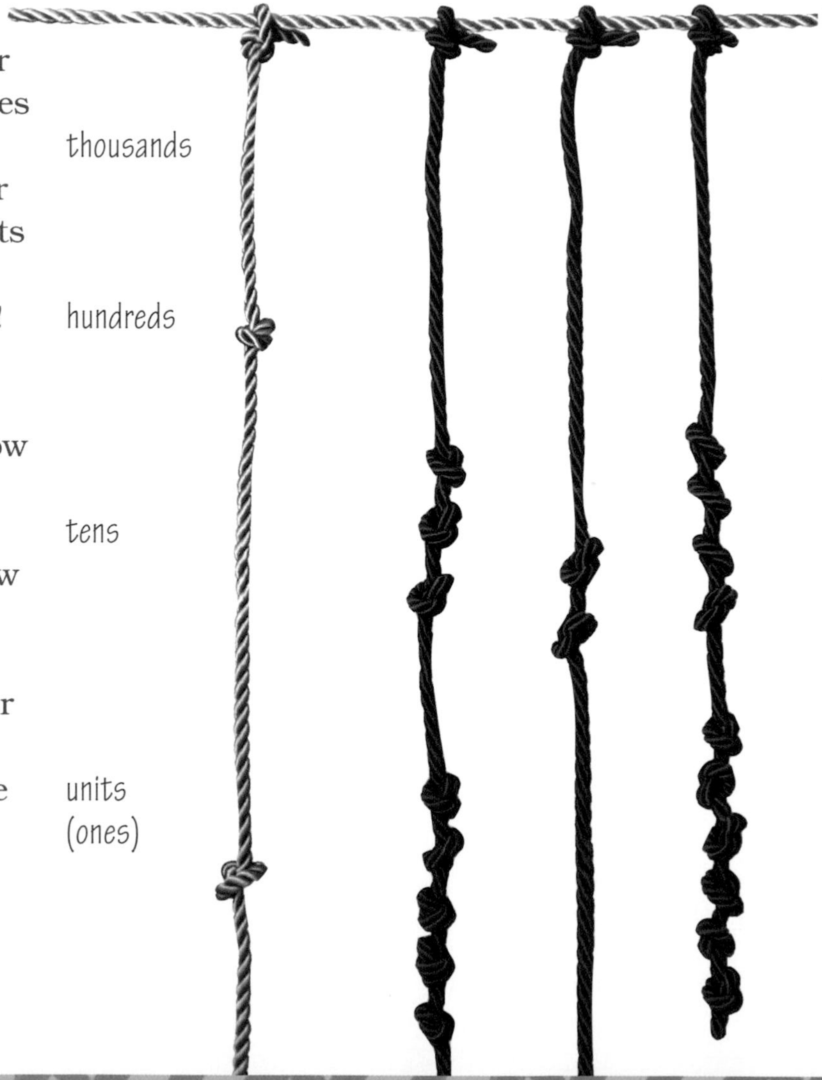

thousands

hundreds

tens

units (ones)

You will need:
- ❖ Three different colors of cord or yarn:
  - ❖ One piece 12" (30 cm) long for the *top cord* (ours is gold)
  - ❖ 3 pieces of another color string (we used red) about 36" (90 cm) long for the *pendant cords*
  - ❖ One piece 36" (90 cm) long of another color string (ours is green) for the *summation cord*

What you do:

1 First, make the blank quipu. Lay the *top cord* horizontally on a flat surface. Then tie the *summation cord* on the left and the three *pendant cords* to the right.

2 Use the pendant cords to record the amounts you want to remember, each on a separate cord. Tie knots onto the correct positions on the cord. Two knots in the tens place, for example, mean 20; six knots in the ones (or units) place represents 6, and so on.

3 Record the total amount of all three numbers ($101, in this example) on the summation string of your quipu.

P.S. If you want to keep your quipu as a piece of art, see the box on this page for a way to frame it.

A Zero?

We write a zero in modern numbers when we want to show that there are none of that number—to show the difference between 3 free tickets (really 03, or no tens and 3 ones) to the movies and 30 tickets (3 tens, or 3 x 10, and no ones), for example. The Inca left a blank space on a quipu when they wanted to show "nothing" in a certain space. Do you think they were starting to see the need for a zero? (See page 90 for more on the zero question.)

How to "frame" your quipu

Even though a quipu was used like a slip of paper to put notations on, yours probably looks more like a piece of interesting art today. To frame it, simply use a piece of thick corrugated cardboard or a corkboard. Spread your quipu out. Then, using sewing pins or pushpins, pin your quipu in place. You can make a frame or just hang your matted quipu on a wall. How many people can figure out what it means?

Quipucamayoc Quest

Feel as if you have mastered the art of quipu-making? Test your quipucamayoc skill by taking on a more challenging project, such as recording the number of kids in your school or the number of relatives you have. You should end up with an amazing-looking quipu, but if you want to go for a new record you'll have to tie a lot of knots. The largest number so far discovered on a real quipu is 97,357! Oh, my aching fingers!

You will need:
❖ Many different colored pieces of yarn

What you do:

1 Collect all the numbers you want to record.

2 Make a blank quipu. To organize your numbers, make groups of cords separated by a little space, and use different colors of cord. (Use one color for each class in one grade, for example, then add another color for each class in the next grade.) Choose a separate color for the summation cord of each category and a summation cord for the whole quipu.

3 Record the numbers on the appropriate cords.

4 Explain your magnificent quipu to someone. Congratulations! You're now an honorary quipucamayoc!

COLORFUL MATH!

FAST-FORWARD

On the quipu, the Inca used different colors and different strings to distinguish between various number data, such as comparing the populations of different villages. Although using color in mathematics may seem unusual, it was (and still is) quite common around the world. The Chinese used red and black rods for counting—the red ones for positive numbers (pluses) and the black ones for negative numbers (minuses). The idea of red and black numbers has even survived into today's business world. Just ask any businessperson if she is "in the red" or "in the black." Today, "red" means losing money or spending more than you are bringing in, so businesspeople tend to feel blue when they are "in the red!"

A Major
Turning Point Ahead

Let's journey on to see what happened when people moved from simply keeping track to writing numerals and counting! Hmmm. Are you curious to know if people went in completely different directions, or if they came up with similar ways of using numbers? Guess we'll have to do some more sleuthing to find out. One thing is for sure: You can count on us to continue the search for the secret life of numbers!

Counting the Roman Way

Where do Roman numerals belong in math's secret life?

Where, oh where?

Where should we put Roman numerals in this book? It seems to us that most people would date Roman numerals back in the time of the Roman Republic, say anywhere from 500 B.C. to 44 B.C., when Julius Caesar was assassinated. In that way of thinking, it belongs right about where the discussion of zero (page 90) is now. But, then again, maybe it belongs here at the end of Part I, as a transition from earlier forms of keeping track. Let's take a closer look.

2000 B.C.   1500 B.C.   1000 B.C.   500 B.C.
(Europe) Italy:
Roman numerals
begin to be used.

IT'S NOT AS EASY AS KNOWING WHEN!

BE A SECRET SUPER SLEUTH

One of the problems as to where to put Roman numerals is that this book isn't about the date that things happened. This is because there wasn't communication between peoples in the earliest times covered in this book. Thus, we can't organize this book *chronologically,* or in the order of years, because, as you know, math moved across the boundaries of time and place in order to survive. And that is part of the mystery of the secret life of math. We are more interested in where Roman numerals belong as far as how numbers developed from using them, first as a means of keeping track, then as a way to record information, and finally, to using them for computation. So, let's start looking at Roman numerals right here!

0   A.D. 500   A.D. 1000   A.D. 1500   A.D. 2000

Europe, Great Britain, Asia, Africa:
Roman numerals
in widespread use.

What's so confusing?

Why is it so difficult to place Roman numerals in the life of math? After all, most historians agree that Rome was built on seven hills in 753 B.C. by Romulus, who named the city after himself. If you remember, Romulus was the surviving twin in "the fight to the finish" with his twin brother, Remus. Talk about sibling rivalry! So, if we know about all of these details, why is it that we don't just place the invention of Roman numerals somewhere in the time of the Romans?

That does make sense, but we have one little thing that bothers us about placing Roman numerals that way. Bear with us, okay? See what you think. Take a look at the Roman numeral for three, for example:

III

Now, think back a bit to some of the earliest ways of keeping track. Remember those hatch marks (pages 16–29)? They spanned time from about 35,000 B.C. all the way to today! Now, how do you show a count of three using hatch marks?

Notice anything? Take a good look at the two things—the Roman numeral for three and the hatch marks for a count of three.

So, what do you observe? And, what do you think? Are Roman numerals an outgrowth of hatch marks from about 34,000 years before the founding of Rome? If people didn't yet know of one another, how did these hatch marks travel in both time and place to where Italy is today over so many years? Could it be possible that Roman numerals existed before Rome? Or, is it a natural progression (since we know

that somehow hatch marks stayed around) to believe that the Romans, who were exceedingly smart, took the hatch marks and then invented a numeral system using them?

And keep in mind that most people would agree that lines for V's and X's are the easiest shapes to carve into bone or wood. So no matter where or when people decided to record numbers on tally sticks, they all used the same kinds of symbols. Some would say that we still use them today and call them Roman numerals.

That type of thinking has led some to believe that the I, V, and X are the oldest kind of writing ever! Yes, even older than any other kind of alphabet or numerals. If that were true, then they would likely be direct followers of the hatch marks used on sticks and found in caves and on cave walls. Now that is very, very old, and that would make you think this discussion of Roman numerals really belongs right after our exploration of hatch marks. Should we move it there?

NO PARROTS NEEDED!

THINK QUICK!

What does the Roman numeral for five remind you of?

Hint: If I ask you to communicate the number for two without speaking or writing, what might you do? What's the possible math link here?

Answer to the question is at the bottom of this page.

Think Quick! answer: Holding up two fingers—especially your two middle fingers—just might remind you of finger counting. Those two fingers sure do look like two Roman numerals for one, as well as the Roman numeral for five. Hmmm!

BE A SECRET SUPER SLEUTH

What's that? What do parrots have to do with sleuthing? Nothing really, except that parrots simply repeat back to you whatever you say to them. And sleuths, or detectives, can't do that if they are to be successful. Historians (and just about anyone else who wants to learn) can't do that, either. The only way to discover the truth is to think and to question. And that's what we need here. Where Roman numerals belong in this book is going to take some careful thought and consideration on your part to come to the best conclusion. And even then, we may not know the real answer, because there is still so much that we don't know from way back then. But what we *can* do is examine what we are aware of at this particular time in the history of humankind, and then we can evaluate it to come to our own best guess.

Polly want a cracker?

Aha! And the answer is...

Write Like a Roman!

TRY THIS!

Use Roman numerals to write the following information on some index cards, and then write the same numbers in Arabic numbers on separate index cards. Shuffle all of the cards together and spread them out face down. Now, play Memory and see if you can match up the same numbers in Roman and Arabic numerals.

❖ your house or apartment number
❖ the grade you are in school
❖ the number of people in your immediate family
❖ your height in inches or centimeters
❖ the year you were born
❖ your phone number
❖ your zip code

To refresh our memories, here's what the Roman numerals look like and what their values are.

I = 1	**C** = 100
V = 5	**D** = 500
X = 10	**M** = 1,000
L = 50	

To read Roman numerals, follow these rules:

When a numeral of equal or lesser value follows a numeral, add them together.
VI = 5 + 1 = 6
XX = 10 + 10 = 20

When a numeral is immediately followed by one of greater value, subtract the first from the second.
IV = 1 from 5 = 4
XL = 10 from 50 = 40
CD = 100 from 500 = 400
CM = 100 from 1,000 = 900

Have any problems? If you have a zero in any of those numbers, you are out of luck! The Roman system, like many other number systems of long ago, did not include a symbol for zero. (See page 90 for more about that.)

CLXXVII

COUNTING THE ROMAN WAY

Break it down

If you are having any trouble decoding Roman numerals, here is a way to do it: Break the numeral down into its parts. Let's say you want to write the year 2968, Roman-style. Break it down; then decode each number and you will have the Roman numeral.

2968 =
2000 + 900 + 60 + 8 =
MM (1000 + 1000) + **CM** (1000 - 100) + **LX** (50 + 10) + **VIII** (5 + 1 + 1 + 1) =
MMCMLXVIII =
2968

FAST-FORWARD

Some historians say that from about 500 B.C. to A.D. 1500, the ancient Romans used I's, V's, and X's—as well as C's, D's, L's, and M's—to write their numbers. Even today, you can often see Roman numerals on many clocks and watch faces, or in the credits at the very end of a movie. Look on the sides of buildings, too, where the year the building was built is often engraved in Roman numerals.

TRY THIS! Go on a Roman numeral treasure hunt. If you can, have all of the players take a disposable camera with them (you can buy them at most grocery stores). Snap a photo when you see a Roman numeral being used. You can click each time or you can click only different kinds of uses. Who found the most Roman numerals?

P.S. If you take your photos carefully, you can make a really nice Roman numeral collage!

(Note: Be sure that an adult accompanies you on your treasure hunt and knows where you are at all times. Thank you.)

Another perspective on computing with Roman numerals

Welcome to ancient Rome! The city of Rome was founded in 753 B.C. and became the center of a powerful empire throughout what are now Europe, Great Britain, and parts of Asia and Africa. In ancient Rome many people lived comfortably in well-planned cities. The ancient Romans engineered and built amazing theaters and buildings, chariot racetracks, huge public baths, and special plumbing called *aqueducts* to bring fresh water to Rome. Have you heard of the saying "All roads lead to Rome"? The Romans also built an incredible road system, including bridges. Clearly, the Romans used Roman numerals to do all of this!

So, you might ask, who are we to say that Roman numerals weren't particularly easy to use and were probably used for keeping track rather than for computations? After all, the brilliant Romans engineered, designed, and built all of these amazing systems. You would be correct to make all of those points. You decide if Roman numerals were too awkward to use.

Keeping track or doing math?

One way to think about all of this is to decide what you think Roman numerals were used for: keeping track of things, as hatch marks were used, or for calculating things, like we use numerals today. Here is a little scheme to help you discover your answer.

Add CLXII + MCCCV. What is your answer—in Roman numerals, of course?

Now, add 2,365 + 3,488. Write your answer in regular Arabic numerals, our Western numbering system. (Answers up the side of this page.)

Which took you the longest? Did you have to rewrite the Roman numerals into Arabic numerals and then put the answer back in Roman numerals again?

Actually, *adding* in Roman numerals is the easiest computation to do with them. You should try multiplying and dividing Roman numerals! So what do you think they were meant to be used for, computations or keeping track?

Given your answer, where do *you* think this section on Roman numerals belongs? At the beginning or end of Part I (KEEPING TRACK), Part II (WRITING IT DOWN), or Part III (FASTER FIGURING)?

Did we choose correctly?

Actually, we went though a similar thought process ourselves. In the end, we decided to put this topic where it would serve to demonstrate our confusion. Many historians believe that Roman numerals were symbols derived from the notched stick markings of ancient peoples and that standardized Roman numerals were modified from these ancient tally markings. Thus, the modern system of Roman numerals was not used until well into Roman times (509 B.C. to A.D. 475). To back this up, historians point out that the earliest known use of the numeral L for 50 is in 44 B.C.

These are very sound arguments, indeed. Yet, we believe Roman numerals don't belong in Part II where numbers were being used for computation, because they were too difficult to work with. And we don't really think they belong right after the discussion of hatch marks, although some historians might make that argument. So, we decided to compromise and place Roman numerals at the end of Part I, but you could very likely make an argument for placing them later in the book.

If you are confused, well, that is a good thing, because it lets you know that being a Super Sleuth is not a matter of right or wrong, but rather a matter of thoughtful consideration. Good job!

Part II

Writing It Down:

Toward a Universal Language

A Major Leap Forward for Humankind

Well, perhaps Einstein was correct that not everything is worth counting, but we humans sure have invented a lot of ways to do just that—and in a lot of different languages, too!

There is not a language in the world today that does not include numerals and words for numbers. Around the world, people seem to have invented similar systems for counting, keeping track, and using numerals, yet the languages we speak are so different.

Why is that? Why would math develop in similar ways across thousands of miles and years, but language went every which way? More precisely, what is it about math that made it almost universal? And how did it happen?

A Clue to the Clues

These questions set the stage for your sleuthing. As we discover the ins and outs of written symbols and try our hand at using counting balls, writing in cuneiform, and then using some hieroglyphs (just for the pure fun of it!), look for the "how" and "why" clues. Try to get a handle on why math developed in similar ways around the globe, but when it came to language, it was every civilization for itself!

Who decided to write things down?

Who actually wrote a number symbol on a piece of clay for the very first time in the history of humankind? Well, that is quite a difficult question. You see, once again we need to think more broadly. So instead of looking for the exact person, we'll ask: Who moved away from the rather broad and clumsy ways of keeping track, such as hatch marks and quipus, to actually putting notations down, much like we write today? And, once again, how and why did people make that change, each in a similar way, although still using whatever natural materials they had around them? After all, this was a giant leap forward. And even more amazing, writing down numbers crossed thousands of years and miles, as if it were a simple thing to have happened. Meanwhile, the life of math remains on a singular track, unlike the multiple tracks of language. What was it that made math and writing down notations such a universal thing even though each pocket of civilization developed independently?

Match these countries to the children counting to three in their native languages.

- Japan
- Germany
- Mexico
- France
- South Africa
- Russia

Un, Deux, Trois

Odin, Dva, Tri

Uno, Dos, Tres

From Pebbles to Symbols

Moving from tokens to written notations

If you live in a city with a subway or metro system, you are likely to be very familiar with tokens. Tokens are basically substitute money. You pay for a token, put it in the subway turnstile, and you are able to enter to ride the subway. It's a very clever system.

Well, guess what? Today's tokens are designed after relics of the very distant past. The huge span of time during which pebbles and stones were used—from about 40,000 B.C. (we are assuming that they were just beginning to be used back then) to the period of 8000 B.C. to 3000 B.C.

40,000 B.C.
Europe, Africa, Middle East:
Pebbles used to track amounts.

30,000 B.C.

20,000 B.C.

MESOPOTAMIA IS HERE

Today's tokens are designed after relics of the very distant past.

(there are many examples of tokens from that period)—sure does make us wonder about the secret to the long life of numbers! For now, let's focus on those tokens found in the area of southwest Asia once called Mesopotamia, the region of the early civilizations of Babylonia, Sumer, Akkad, and Assyria (now all part of the Middle East).

How do you think today's subway tokens got started so long ago and survived to now? Finding the answer—or at least making an "educated guess" (that means you have good background information but you can't prove it yet with "hard"—the kind you can hold in your hand and say "See!"—evidence) is our job as sleuths. How did an idea get all the way from then to now?

Middle East:
Specific clay
tokens represent
amounts.
3500 B.C.

8000 B.C.
Middle East:
Earliest clay tokens
symbolize items.

3300 B.C.
Middle East:
Earliest form of
written numerals.

0

A.D. 10,000

CALCULATING CLUE

BE A SECRET SUPER SLEUTH

There are going to be clues flying right and left in this section of our search for math's mysterious secret life, but let me just say one word: *Calculate.* No, let's make that two words: *Calculate* and *calculus.* More precisely, get this: The Latin word for "pebble" is *calculus.* Aha!

P.S. Latin was the language of the ancient Romans whom you just visited on pages 48 to 55.

FAST-FORWARD

Have you ever made something of clay, and then had it fired (baked) in a kiln until it was hard? If you have, we're guessing that at least once after finishing a baked clay hand-made object, your clay masterpiece got knocked off a shelf or dropped on the floor, and . . . crash! Your clay object had broken into more pieces than Humpty Dumpty. Sound familiar? Here's our quandary: How do you suppose these clay tokens made anywhere from 10,000 to 5,000 years ago are still being found today?

1032 x 347!

1032 x 347?

And we're off!

In 8000 B.C. there were still no written numbers, but people had gotten pretty good at keeping track using pebbles, shells, bones, or other small things available to them, in addition to using tallies or fingers. But as cities formed and flourished, and as trade between them began to expand—well, can you imagine hauling around thousands of pebbles to keep track of what people bought or owed?

You see, Mesopotamia was the site of some of the oldest civilizations, starting out as a cluster of villages and then turning into larger urban areas. The people traded and used metal tools such as saws to build innovations including—ta-da!—the wheel. (Yes, it's finally here! Although we are not sure what group of people invented the wheel, the oldest wheel found as of now is believed to be 5,500 years old and was found in Mesopotamia.)

In this region, clay was easily found, shaped, and dried. Archaeologists have found thousands and thousands of clay tokens used from about 8000 B.C. to 3000 B.C., when trading became quite brisk in this region. Some tokens were very simply shaped objects; many were in geometrical shapes. Some were used in a similar way to early hatch marks: One token equals one item. Others stood for varying amounts depending on their shapes. And some, from about 3500 B.C. to 3300 B.C., were even found grouped inside *clay counting balls.*

PEBBLE POCKETS

MAKE IT REAL

Well, maybe you *can't* really imagine what it would be like doing transactions with a couple of hundred pebbles hauled around in your pockets, after all! It would be a lot heavier than the same number of pennies (and you probably know how annoying a pocketful of pennies can be). Just for the fun of it, gather together about a hundred pebbles (or as many as you can find). Wearing a pair of old pants or shorts, stuff the pebbles in as many pockets as possible. Then, just leave them there for the day. What do you think, eh? In this case, they probably are not "worth their weight in gold," as the saying goes!

NOT JUST CIRCLES!

MAKE IT REAL

A lot of people living in the U.S. might think that all tokens are round, because all of the coins used as money in the U.S. are round. But that is not the case the world over. Countries such as China, Aruba, and the United Arab Emirates have coins in varied shapes. We wonder where that idea came from?

In ancient China you could have used the square hole in the middle of these ancient coins to thread them together and keep them safely around your neck. Today you could easily get one of these small hexagonal five fils coins as change in the United Arab Emirates or fifty pence coins in England.

Good-bye to pockets full of pebbles!

When you have a group of similar items, what do you usually do? If you said that you find a way to store them together, such as by using a rubber band, a shoe box, or an envelope, then you and these ancient peoples think alike. Some very clever accountants in the Mesopotamia region thought to store their tokens according to the type of transaction. Tokens representing, for example, the number of sheep sent to graze for the summer were placed in a *counting ball*—a hollow ball made out of clay that could be sealed shut and kept safe over periods of time. When the herd came back at summer's end, the ball was broken open, revealing the tokens, and the record-keeper could make sure all the sheep had returned. It was an ingenious counting and record-keeping system!

These clay counting tokens (calculi) are from 3300 B.C. The counting balls were about the size of a tennis ball.

Record It in a Counting Ball!

TRY THIS!

No paper and pencil? Make a counting ball and counting tokens to keep your records organized. Then, imagine what you would think of this new invention if the alternative were to carry around heaps of pebbles!

You will need:
- ❖ Salt Clay (see recipe) or modeling clay, for tokens
- ❖ Balloon
- ❖ Newspaper, torn into 1" x 4" (2.5 x 10 cm) strips
- ❖ Papier-Mâché Paste (see recipe)
- ❖ Brown paint
- ❖ Paintbrush
- ❖ Masking tape

Salt Clay:
- ❖ 2 cups (500 ml) flour
- ❖ 1 cup (250 ml) salt
- ❖ ¾ to 1 cup (175 to 250 ml) water
- ❖ 2 tablespoons (25 ml) vegetable oil

In a bowl, mix together the flour and salt. Slowly add the water and the oil to the flour mix. Stir until dough forms.

Papiér-Mâché Paste:

- ❖ ¹⁄₂ cup (125 ml) flour
- ❖ ¹⁄₂ cup (125 ml) water

Stir the flour and water together in a bowl. The paste should look thick and creamy. Add more water or flour, if necessary. Store in a container in the refrigerator until ready to use.

What you do to make the tokens:

Make a different token shape out of the Salt Clay or modeling clay for each kind of item for which you want to keep a record. (For example, one token shape for the books you read this month and another token shape for the times you mowed the lawn.)

What you do to make the counting ball:

1 Slip the different tokens inside the balloon; then, blow it up.

2 Cover the inflated balloon with strips of newspaper dipped in the Papiér-Mâché Paste, overlapping the strips. Build up several layers, leaving a small hole where the balloon is tied. Let them dry.

3 Paint your counting ball to look like it is made of clay. Let dry. Pop the balloon and remove the balloon bits, throwing every bit away.* Tape over the small opening to seal the ball shut. Later, when you want to remember how many books you've read, open the counting ball and take out the tokens.

Warning: Balloons and pieces of balloons are very dangerous for young children. It takes just a small piece for a child to choke. Please check very carefully that every piece of balloon or any extra balloons are thrown away immediately. Thank you.

3-D Tokens Morph to 2-D Symbols!

Still, there was a problem with those clay "envelopes": You couldn't see what was inside once they were sealed! At some point, someone decided to press the token symbols into the outside of the clay ball before the clay dried to remember what was inside … and—in about 3300 B.C.—the idea of using symbols to show numbers was born! Although not like the numbers we use today, the idea of writing symbols to show amounts had begun.

For a while—from 3300 B.C. to 3200 B.C.—people used solid counting balls with notations on the outside. Then, around 3200 B.C. to 3100 B.C., the Sumerians made the giant leap to using number symbols on slabs of clay, and it was soon good-bye to counting balls. Imagine! Something could become obsolete in 3100 B.C.!

FOCUS ON "OBSOLETE"

BE A SECRET SUPER SLEUTH

We think that the idea of counting balls becoming obsolete way back in 3100 B.C. must be a major clue. After all, keeping track of things was coming along just fine. So, here are our clues for you:

Clue #1: Why do things become obsolete?

Clue #2: What could that have to do with the secret life of numbers?

Are any bells going off in your head? Do you think you are getting close to what controls the mysterious secret life of numbers? Don't tell if you do. Just keep your thoughts to yourself and test them out against what happens next.

Imagine! Something could become obsolete in 3100 B.C.!

TRY THIS! Ask someone about your grandparents' ages how many things they can think of that have become obsolete, or out of date. Do they have anything in the attic or basement that they can show you?

Are we there yet?

Well, Super Sleuths, we've made some progress here. We've moved from the simplest methods of keeping track to a very early method of notation, using symbols, wet clay, and a stylus. It feels downright modern—and it is only about 3200 B.C.!

Using Cuneiform

A step backward—or not?

The life of math seems to be progressing nicely. But let's not get lulled into thinking that everything moved along in a *linear* fashion—that is, everything moved from one year to the next, making progress as the years went by. That was *not* the case in the secret life of math. No way! The years would move along, but remember that these were still separate civilizations that encompassed pockets of people who had minimal, if any, contact with other cultures. What one group invented was not passed along to

40,000 B.C.   30,000 B.C.   20,000 B.C.

another group. It wasn't as if they could teach one another what they discovered or invented. *Au contraire, mon ami!** (Just checking to see if you are still there!)

People of each group had to invent their number systems

*Translated from French: *To the contrary, my friend!*

themselves. And that is where the secret comes in. How is it that very similar number systems developed, invented by different peoples, in different times, often separated by thousands of miles

and thousands of years? What is the—to use a math term—*common denominator* that kept numbers and math moving ahead? That common denominator, or common element, will solve the mystery of how numbers have survived from the cave dwellers to today!

Middle East:
Archaic numbers on clay
slabs develop in Sumer.
3200 B.C.

10,000 B.C.   2700 B.C.   0   A.D. 10,000
Middle East:
Cuneiform numbers
introduced.

Please pass in your homework!

Here's a case in point. It is now the year 2700 B.C., 500 years after the first use of clay tablets by the Sumerians. It's an ordinary day, with the children—boys only, still!—in school.

The Babylonians also recorded numbers in a rather "bulky" way. They adopted the special kind of writing from the Sumerians called *cuneiform* (coon-EE-a-form) that they engraved on slabs of wet clay, using the shaped end of a reed as a writing tool, or stylus. (The word *cuneiform* means "wedge-shaped" and refers to both the letters and numbers used.)

Boys in wealthy families went to schools called *edubbas*, meaning "tablet houses." They did their work on these clay tablets. Whenever written work needed to be saved, the clay tablet was dried in the sun or baked in an oven fueled by animal manure. (Oh my! No wonder kids might have forgotten to "save" their homework!) Can you imagine how hard it must have been to carry your homework home on those days when the teacher

(Math) all seemed to happen in spurts of growth and spurts of repetition. That it happened at all is what we are curious about, because that kept math alive.

"piled on the work"?

Does all this sound somewhat familiar to what was done when the people who lived in Sumer moved from counting balls to tablets in about 3200 B.C.? Well, you are right. That was in a different time but there you have it! How could this have happened? The idea of the tablet and the writing stylus sure do sound alike.

This is an actual clay tablet that was used in 2100 B.C. to calculate an area of land.

©Erich Lessing/Art Resource, NY/Louvre, Paris, France

COUNTING IN CUNEIFORM

The Babylonian number system, which developed from the earlier form of writing numbers, was a *sexagesimal* system, which means it was based on the number 60 that, when written in cuneiform, looks sort of like a Y or wedge shape. The number 10 had its own symbol in cuneiform. It looked sort of like a hook.

Cuneiform numbers 1 through 10:

1	Y	6	
2	YY	7	
3	YYY	8	
4		9	
5		10	

Can you guess what the numbers 11 and 12 looked like? Think "hooks," "wedges," or Y's.

11

12

And 20? Two hooks. (Hey, this is easy!)

20

You get the idea. Numbers 1 to 59 followed the same system. After that, it got a little trickier: The wedge symbol could represent 1 or 60, depending on where it was placed in relation to the other number symbols. (This is where the *sexagesimal*, or "based on the number 60," idea comes in.)

60

The number 61 would be written like this, with a wedge for the sixties place and a wedge in the ones place.

61

Can you tell what this number is?

Let's see ... the symbols for 60 and 10 and 2. Add them together and you get the number 72! (For more on cuneiform numbers, see page 92.)

THINK QUICK!

How about decoding this cuneiform number?

Answer to the question is up the side of this page.

Think Quick! answer: YY *means 2 x 60,* ◄ *is 10 and* YYY *is 7. Thus, 120 + 10 + 7 = 137!*

Create a

The longer we wait, the more we learn!
Isn't it interesting that the further away from the time something took place—even thousands of years later—the more we seem to eventually learn? Of course, that is not always true, but thanks to serious researchers and Super Sleuths like you, and now with advanced technology such as carbon dating, we are learning more about the ancients as the years go by. For instance, there is some evidence being found of ancient trade routes and therefore some minimal contact between ancient cultures. The "incense road" (where incense was traded) that connected Egypt with Arabia and the Indies is now thought to have been in existence since at least 1800 B.C.

THINK QUICK!

Can you figure out the birth date on the cuneiform birthday tablet we've made?

Answer to the question is up the side of this page.

TRY THIS! Take the Babylonian challenge and make your own cuneiform birthday tablet!

You will need:
❖ Newspaper, to protect work surface
❖ Salt Clay (see recipe)
❖ Waxed paper
❖ Red and green food coloring
❖ Rolling pin or glass jar
❖ Pencil
❖ Paper

Salt Clay:
❖ 2 cups (500 ml) flour
❖ 1 cup (250 ml) salt
❖ ¾ to 1 cup (175 to 250 ml) water
❖ 2 tablespoons (25 ml) vegetable oil

In a bowl, mix together the flour and salt. Slowly add the water and the oil to the flour mix. Stir until dough forms.

Cuneiform Birthday Tablet

What you do:

1 Spread the newspaper over your work surface. Soften the clay by kneading it with your hands for a minute or so. Working on waxed paper, add a few drops of the food coloring to get the brown tablet color.

2 Roll out the clay so that it is roughly oval shaped and about ½" (1 cm) thick.

3 Write the month and day you were born on paper in cuneiform numbers. Once you are certain you have the correct numbers, use the pencil as a *stylus* (the original writing tool) to make cuneiform shapes by pressing into the clay.

4 Allow the clay to dry for at least two days in a sunny place, or ask permission to bake it in the oven at 300°F (150°C) until hardened. Then, say happy birthday with your cuneiform tablet!

THINK QUICK!

Something's missing

Do you notice anything missing in the cuneiform numeral system?

Here's a hint: Some might say
what is missing is very, very important;
others might say
it is a whole lot of nothing.

Answer to the question is up the side of this page.

Let's call it "Vacationatus"

The Babylonians depended on planting crops to give them most of their food. To do this, they needed to know when to plant seeds and when to harvest the crops to make the most of the growing season. So the Babylonians invented a calendar that alternated between a 29- and 30-day-month schedule. The year was 12 months long, or 354 days. Because a real year is actually just over 365 days (as we know now, but they didn't know then), over time the calendar would become less and less accurate. The ancient Babylonian king would, therefore, order a new month every so often when the calendar got too far off track. When would you order the new month? During summer vacation, we bet!

Using Cuneiform: A Step Backward–or Not?

We've just taken a glimpse on our back-in-time sleuthing adventure at one example of how math didn't just keep moving forward one year after another. It all seemed to happen in spurts of growth and spurts of repetition. That it happened at all is what we are curious about, because that kept math alive.

Was math taking a step backward or a step forward with cuneiform numbers? To our way of thinking, based on what we know, it doesn't really seem to be either. (In fact, it seems we are asking the wrong question, which we have found can be a real stumbling block to solving a dilemma.)

• Math was neither going forward nor stepping backward.
• Using cuneiform was neither good nor bad.
• Math was neither making progress nor marking time.

It just was.

The use of cuneiform written on tablets 500 years after the first tablets with symbols were used just shows us that the life of math continued. Why or how? Well, we each need to look beneath the surface of the facts to find the secret to its survival.

Hieroglyphics

Using pictures to write and keep track

Since we've been leaping around the world in time and place, allow us please to further confuse you. It is still around the year 2000 B.C. We are in northern Africa, in what is called Egypt today, along the Nile River. But when we take a look at the secret life of math here, we discover that it is going through a major growth spurt! What's up with that?

3500 B.C.

3000 B.C.
(North Africa)
Egypt: Hieroglyphic
numbers in use.

2500 B.C.

About 1850 B.C.
(North Africa)
Egypt: Original
Rhind papyrus
written.

1500 B.C.
(North Africa)
Egypt: Hieroglyphic
numbers found on
stone carving.

(North Africa)
Egypt: Rhind
papyrus copied
by Ahmose.
1650 B.C.

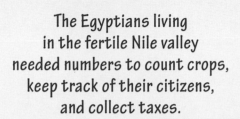

The Egyptians living
in the fertile Nile valley
needed numbers to count crops,
keep track of their citizens,
and collect taxes.

It's all about decoding!

"I can't read that. It looks like it was written in hieroglyphics!" Have you ever said that? Usually we mean that we have no way of understanding what is being written because we don't know what the written symbols mean.

But we are about to change that, as we discover the secret life of *hieroglyphics.* By 3000 B.C., the Egyptians living in the fertile Nile valley needed numbers to count crops, keep track of their citizens, and collect taxes for the *pharaoh,* or leader. So they invented *hieroglyphics,* a system of writing that uses pictorial symbols, called *hieroglyphs* (HI-row-glifs), or just *glyphs.*

500 B.C.   0   A.D. 500   A.D. 1000   A.D. 1500   A.D. 1858
(Europe) Scotland:
A. Henry Rhind
purchases
Rhind papyrus.

Ancient School Days

What was school like in ancient Egypt? Well, going to school cost money, so most Egyptians never learned to read, to write, or to use numbers and understand math. Usually, only the sons of powerful people had the opportunity to go to school. (Sorry to say, no girls were allowed.) The students used very different writing materials for their math problems back then. To record lessons, they used a wooden tablet covered with plaster. To write, they used a special paintbrush with red and black ink. The tablet could be wiped clean after each use, ready to be used again.

Usually, only the sons of powerful people had the opportunity to go to school. (Sorry to say, no girls were allowed.)

EGYPTIAN NUMBERS

BE A SECRET SUPER SLEUTH

Egyptians had been using finger counting since 2500 B.C., or earlier. The first Egyptian number system, however, used *hieroglyphs* (HI-row-glifs), numbers based on picture symbols. Another system that came along later (and was much more convenient) was called *hieratic*, meaning "sacred," because Egyptian priests invented it. This is the system that was used to write on papyrus (see page 82).

1
(stroke)

10
(cattle hobble)

100
(coil of rope)

Hieroglyphic Handiwork

The ancient Egyptians used hieroglyphs to write their numbers, just as they used drawings to make up the written Egyptian language. There were distinct characters to represent 1, 10, 100, 1,000, and so on up to 10,000,000! (Don't worry, they didn't have to memorize ten million different glyphs. The characters were simply repeated.) Below are the main symbols used for numbers up to a million.

"Pretty easy, right? To read these numbers simply find the value of each of the symbols and add them up. For example, two coils of rope equal 200. Five tadpoles equal 500,000. To make things easier, first find the value of the symbols having the greatest value. Then, keep adding all the symbols to decipher the Egyptian number."

THINK QUICK!

These two numbers are shown on a stone carving from Karnak, dating around 1500 B.C., now displayed in the Louvre.

Answer to the question is up the side of this page.

1,000
(lotus plant)

10,000
(finger)

100,000
(tadpole)

1,000,000
(a god with arms supporting the sky)

Think Quick! answer: The numbers are 276 and 4622. How did you do?

Papyrus—a kind of paper product

For very important documents where the information needed to be saved, *papyrus* was used, but usually the practice draft was composed on the wooden tablet first. (The word *paper* comes from the word *papyrus,* even though paper isn't really made from papyrus.) Papyrus paper was made by weaving stalks of the papyrus marsh weed that grew on the banks of the Nile River. Layers of the woven strips were soaked in water, pounded with a mallet, and left to dry in the sun. Once dry, the surface was scraped smooth and the papyrus "paper" was ready to write on. (Papyrus feels more like rough cardboard than writing paper to us, though.) To give proper credit, the very first paper was not made in the land now called Egypt, but was invented in China, where one of the oldest pieces can be seen today in a museum in Xian. Of course, that shouldn't surprise us! It is just one more example of math having many lives that seemed to repeat themselves in faraway places and times.

ANOTHER IMPORTANT CLUE

BE A SECRET SUPER SLEUTH

What do you suppose the Egyptian students used to "take notes" or to write things they wanted to remember? (After all, if they wiped the tablet clean each time, they would have to wipe away their notes.) The answer to this—in a way—is a clue to how and why humans the world over invented things—including numbers and math!

Maya Glyphs in Central America!

While the Egyptian use of glyphs was certainly much earlier, the Maya (MY-uh), who lived in what is now southern Mexico and parts of Central America, also used glyphs, beginning in about A.D. 250. That was the height of the *El Mundo Maya,* the ancient Maya empire that helped this amazing civilization of long ago to prosper.

In most villages, the Maya rulers, who were mathematical astronomer priests, governed the people. These rulers came up with incredible number systems that were mostly organized in groups of 20. (Could this number have been chosen because it is related to our 20 digits—our fingers, thumbs, and toes?)

Maya-Style Numbers

System One
One number system the Maya used was a series of symbols

combined with pictures of heads (glyphs) of gods like the ones shown on the side of this stela carved in A.D. 731. There were 19 head glyphs in all, representing the 13 gods of the Superior World, with six variations. A separate head glyph represented zero. This special system of head glyphs was used only for special occasions, and you can understand why: Writing out numbers was literally like drawing portraits, a real form of "art"—a lot different than writing out our numbers today!

System Two

Although the glyph numbers are fun to look at, we think you will agree that the second number system of the Maya was much more practical. This second system was based on a pattern of dots and bars, with a shell symbol used to represent the Maya idea of "nothing," or zero. (Some historians think that

the shell that represents the Maya zero symbolized an empty oyster shell. Oysters were served on shell halves at important feasts. Empty shells meant no oysters, or "nothing!" How clever is that?)

a shell = 0
a dot = 1
a bar = 5

In different positions, these symbols could represent numbers up to infinity, not unlike our own system! Sound a little tricky? It's actually easy, once you get the hang of it.

TRY THIS!

Here are the Maya numbers from zero to 11:

0 — (shell)
1 — •
2 — • •
3 — • • •
4 — • • • •
5 — ▬
6 — • over ▬
7 — • • over ▬
8 — • • • over ▬
9 — • • • • over ▬
10 — ▬ over ▬
11 — • over ▬ over ▬

Can you guess what number this is?

Let's see . . . two bars and four dots—that's 5 + 5 + 1 + 1 + 1 + 1. You've got it; it's 14! Great! Why don't we try another one?

Three bars, meaning 5 + 5 + 5. Wow! Now you are counting like the Maya!

For numbers above 19, the counting got a little trickier. (For more about Maya numbers, see pages 90 to 96.)

WILL THE REAL INVENTOR PLEASE RECEIVE CREDIT?

FAST-FORWARD

The *Rhind papyrus* is an important record of 87 ancient Egyptian math problems. It was written by a scribe named Ahmose, who copied it in 1650 B.C. from an older document, written about 200 years earlier. The Rhind papyrus is named after the Scotsman, A. Henry Rhind, who purchased it in 1858 and realized its importance. Now it is also referred to as the *Ahmes papyrus*, after the scribe Ahmose who copied it from an unknown author. Some people feel that the name Ahmes papyrus gives credit to the person who most deserves it. Who do you think—Ahmes, or Rhind, or the unnamed earlier scribe—should have his name associated with this famous and valuable math document?

THINK QUICK!

In the paragraph "Will the real inventor please receive credit?" why isn't the date 1858 marked either B.C. or A.D.?

Answer to the question is up the side of this page.

You are looking at the mathematical "Rhind" (or "Ahmes") papyrus that was created about 1650 B.C. in Thebes, Egypt!

©HIP/Art Resource, NY/British Museum, London, Great Britain

Think Quick! answer: The date couldn't be B.C. because the Rhind papyrus couldn't have been purchased, as it wouldn't have been written yet! So it goes without saying that we're talking about A.D. time here.

SEVEN CATS . . . AND MORE!

MAKE IT REAL

Try to solve problem 79 on the Rhind/Ahmes papyrus. Figure it out in hieroglyphics for a greater challenge, using numerals on a piece of scrap paper for a little less challenge, or use a calculator for the easiest method by far. No matter which method you use, read the problem carefully and don't peek at the answer at the bottom of this page.

Seven houses each have seven cats. The seven cats each kill seven mice. If not for the cats, each of the mice would have eaten seven ears of wheat. Each ear of wheat would have produced seven measures of flour. How many measures of flour did the cats save?

Many years later, a traveler took the "seven cats" idea from the Rhind/Ahmes papyrus and introduced a similar problem in Europe, in the form of a poem that you may have heard:

As I was going to St. Ives,
I met a man with seven wives.
Every wife had seven sacks.
Every sack had seven cats.
Every cat had seven kits.
Kits, cats, sacks and wives,
How many were going to St. Ives?

Fractions...Already?

By the year 1800 B.C., Egyptians were using unit fractions! Why do you think the very clever Egyptians invented these? (Another clue to the secret to math's life.) The Egyptians were considered very advanced for using the fractions ½, ¼, ⅛, 1/16, 1/32, 1/64 in a diagram called the *Eye of Horus.*

Who's Horus and what did he have to do with fractions? This picture shows the eye of Horus, son of Osiris, one of Egypt's principal gods. (The name Horus was associated with kings, who were thought to be godlike. When a king died, he became Osiris, and the new ruler became Horus.) The eye represents 1 hekat (unit) of grain and is considered a good-luck symbol. By today's standards, 1 hekat of grain is the equivalent to about 4.8 liters, or approximately 5 quarts. That's a little over a gallon, or just over the amount that fits in a gallon milk jug.

Make an Eye

TRY THIS! Each of the parts of the Eye of Horus is a hieroglyphic symbol for one of the fractions in the series ½, ¼, ⅛, 1/16, 1/32, and 1/64. Cleverly arranged, these symbols make the Eye of Horus.

# of Horus Amulet

You will need:

❖ Newspaper, to protect the work surface

❖ Scrap paper and pencil

❖ Cardboard

❖ White craft glue

❖ Small bowl or clean container for mixing glue

❖ Water

❖ Tissue paper

❖ Gold spray paint (or yellow if gold is not available), or gold or yellow tempera paint and a paintbrush

❖ Scissors, to cut finished amulet

❖ Nail, to make a hole

❖ Ribbon, yarn, or piece of leather, to make a necklace

What you do:

1 Practice drawing the fraction hieroglyphs on a piece of scrap paper. When you are comfortable, draw the Eye of Horus on your piece of cardboard.

2 Prepare the glue in the container by mixing it in thirds: 2 parts glue plus 1 part water. Tear off pieces of the tissue paper and moisten them in the glue mixture.

3 Form the tissue into "snakes" and place these strips over the lines you've drawn on the cardboard. You will have a raised Eye of Horus design. Use plenty of the glue mixture to attach the tissue.

4 Allow the design to dry for a day or two. When dry, take it outdoors to spray-paint it gold (or yellow). If indoors, just paint it with paint and a brush.

5 Cut out the amulet, punch a hole through the top using a nail. String it on a piece of yarn, ribbon, or leather, and wear the necklace for good luck!

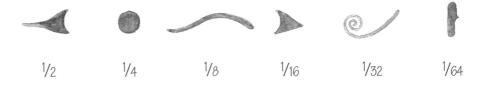

| ½ | ¼ | ⅛ | 1/16 | 1/32 | 1/64 |

Think Quick! answer: If you add these fractions up, you will notice that they don't quite add up to 1 whole. There is 1/64 missing. According to legend, the scribe who pointed this out was awarded 1/64 of all the grain in the land known as Egypt. Imagine! The scribe, now rich, must have jumped for joy!

THINK QUICK!

Do you notice anything strange about the series of fractions in the Eye of Horus?

Here's a clue: Add them up. (Remember to use a common denominator of 64, so 1/32, for example, would equal 2/64.) Discover anything now?

Answer to the question is up the side of this page.

A Civilization Ahead of Its Time

Whoa! How'd we advance so quickly? Well, not everyone *did* advance so quickly. While people of ancient Europe were living in Stone Age (primitive) conditions, the people of ancient Egypt were wearing fine linens, devising calendars and an intricate writing system based on pictures, and growing grains like barley and corn that could be stored for hard times.

Ancient Egypt was so advanced for its time! Egyptian doctors performed brain surgery (successfully!), Egyptians built the pyramids, and people prospered and worked hard in the fields. It all serves to remind us, however, that communication between various cultures was not very efficient. Information about what one community of peoples did was mostly *not* shared with other cultural groups, even though there is evidence that there was some trading at this time.

And that raises a puzzling question for all serious detectives: If math was not passed along from one civilization to another, how did it survive?

Forward or Back?

Now that we've seen how quickly one civilization moved ahead, it is important to remind ourselves that most civilizations at this time were, well, far from civilized. And since these civilizations did not interact with one another, they had a lot of catching up to do if the secret life of math were to continue moving ahead.

And that raises a puzzling question for all serious detectives: If math was not passed along from one civilization to another, how did it survive?

Zip, Zephirum, Zero
Why bother with nothing?

It isn't really all that curious that ancient peoples, for the most part, weren't interested in zero. Why bother with nothing? After all, would you want zero ice cream, zero popcorn at the movies, zero recess, or even worse, zero vacation? You'd be hard-pressed to find someone who would say, "Oh, please, please, give me a zero on the test!" The same held true for most civilizations: Zero was a no-show when it came to numbering systems.

While including zero as a number might seem to make perfect sense to us today, remember that it had to be invented in order for it to be used. And it had to be used a lot to survive. It seems that many ancient civilizations thought "zero" about zero.

Middle East: Babylonians use 2 wedge-shaped marks to mean empty space to differentiate numbers. 400 B.C.

2000 B.C.   1500 B.C.   1000 B.C.   700 B.C.   400 B.C.

700 B.C. Middle East: Babylonians use 3 hook marks to indicate empty space in number.

400 B.C. (Asia) China: Use of empty space to differentiate numbers.

BANISHING ZERO?

MAKE IT REAL

Imagine life without zero. How would you record the difference between receiving a $1 or $10 allowance? How would you indicate that you aced a quiz and got a 90—not a 9! And when someone hands you $1.00 in change when it was supposed to be $10.00—well, exactly how would you explain that?

TRY THIS! For a whole day, try not to use a zero in numerals or numbers, nor the word zero in conversation, nor any other word that means zero in your language. (So if someone asks you if you would like extras on peas and broccoli, no fair saying, "Actually, I don't want any," or "None, please," because that is the same as saying zero.)

(Asia) India:
Aryabhata develops place-value number system.
A.D. 500

(Asia) India:
First concrete evidence that Indian mathematicians recognize zero as a real value.
A.D. 876

0

A.D. 665
Central America:
Maya use zero in place-value number system.

A.D. 1000   A.D. 1200
(Europe) Italy:
Leonardo Fibonacci spreads use of zero in Europe.

A.D. 1600
Europe:
Zero used by most peoples of Europe.

A.D. 2000

Uh-oh! Something's wrong here!

Remember the clever people who lived in what is now part of the Middle East who developed a whole system of numerals called *cuneiform*? (See page 72.) It seemed like everything made sense when writing in cuneiform, right? Well, not exactly. If you remember, they had numbers for 1 through 59; then they began all over again for 60. Big problem! You see, there was no way to tell the difference between 1 and 60, unless you knew what the numbers referred to or the spacing of the other written numbers.

If you left a note for your Mom back then (written on a tablet, of course), telling her that you ate one (1) fig, what would she think? Did you eat all 60 figs that were set aside for guests? Or, did you just help yourself to 1 fig? The cuneiform wedge symbol could mean both of these numbers.

The rule of position

A number's value depended on its *situation,* or place, in the number. Mathematicians refer to that as the *rule of position*.

The rule of position was discovered at different times in the history of the world. For example, the Babylonians, the Chinese, the Maya peoples, and the people of India all developed positional number systems. Then, with the rule of position as the basis for a method of recording numbers, it was soon realized that a zero was needed. Different cultures developed the idea of zero, though often in a different form (more of a placeholder) than the zero we know today.

At first, zero was not thought of as an actual value. Instead, it was either ignored completely, or a space or symbol was used to show an empty position in a number. For example, by 700 B.C. in Babylonia, zero was used only to show how the two and six were related. Zero as a number didn't exist. By 400 B.C., the Chinese were using an empty space to show the difference between a number like 2 or 20. In India, a heavy dot was used to mark an empty number position. (It wasn't until A.D. 876 that we have concrete evidence that Indian mathematicians recognized zero as a real value!)

The Inca left a blank space on a quipu (see page 45) when they wanted to show "nothing." The Maya in what is now southern Mexico and Central America were on top of things in A.D. 665 when they included a real zero in their number system despite their earlier knowledge about zero. Believe it or not, zero didn't appear in Europe

> It isn't really all that curious that ancient peoples, for the most part, weren't interested in zero. Why bother with nothing?

until about A.D. 1200! Even then, the City Council in Florence, Italy, did not welcome zero with open arms. They said that it would be too easy to make a zero into a 6 or 9, and so they made using zero against the law! It wasn't for another 400 years that using *zephirum* became common in Europe.

Numbers, Take Your Places!

Let's compare the Maya system and our present-day system. Both are *place value* number systems. That means the number symbols, or *digits* (the 1, 2, or 3, or the dots and bars), have different values depending on what position they occupy in a number. For instance, what would you rather have, 4 free rides at an amusement park, or 40? How about 400! (See? It's the same digit 4, but in a different *place*.)

The Maya used the same idea with their dot and bar digits, except that the place-value positions were listed up and down, not sideways! Reading from top to bottom, here's the number for 447, Maya-style (remember, the Maya number system was based on 20):

1 dot in the *four hundreds* place, or 1 x 400 = 400

2 dots in the *twenties* place, or 2 x 20 = 40

a bar and 2 dots in the *units* (ones) place, or 5 + 2 = 7

Put it all together, and you get 400 + 40 + 7, or 447!

THINK QUICK!

Ready for a challenge? Try this one:

Answer to the question is up the side of this page.

Think Quick! answer: From the bottom, 4 dots in the units place = 4; the shell symbol in the twenties place means no 20, that is it means zero; and 2 dots and 1 bar in the four hundreds place means 7 x 400, or 2,800. So 4 + 2,800 = 2,804!

Munchin' Maya Number Cookies

TRY THIS!

Let's make a batch of Maya Number Cookies, based on the place values we've just seen in use. And since Maya number systems were based on a base of 20, let's make a batch of 20 cookies!

You will need:
- One 1.55-ounce (43 g) chocolate bar
- Zip-locking bag
- Bowl
- 1 package ready-made sugar cookie dough
- Mixing spoon
- Waxed paper
- Rolling pin or glass jar
- Cookie sheet or large baking pan
- Icing (homemade or store-bought) to "glue" decorations onto each cookie
- Malt balls or other small round candies for the dots
- Black or red licorice pieces for the bars

What you do:

1 Preheat oven to 350°F (180°C). Place the unwrapped chocolate bar in the zip-locking bag and crush it until it resembles coarse crumbs.

2 Put the prepared cookie dough and chocolate crumbs into the bowl. Mix lightly.

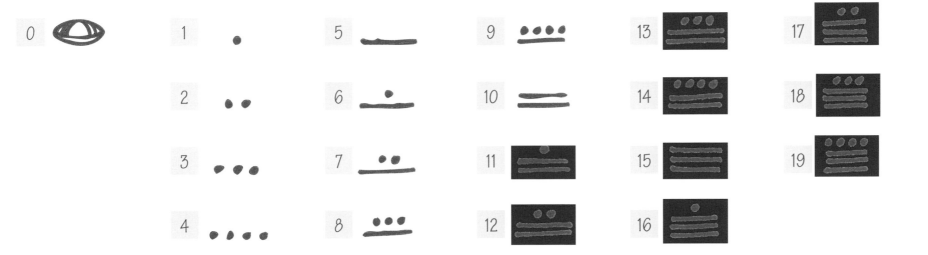

3 Place a portion of the dough between two pieces of waxed paper. Roll out the dough so that it's about ½" (1 cm) thick.

4 Cut the dough into rectangular-shaped cookies and place each on the cookie sheet. Leave about 2" (5 cm) of space between each cookie.

5 Bake the cookies according to the package directions.

6 Remove the cookie sheet from the oven. Cool the cookies on a rack for at least 30 minutes. Use icing to "glue" the candy decorations onto the cookies to construct Mayan numerals. Each cookie should have one Maya number on it, and each cookie eater has to try to figure out what that number is!

THE DECI-DECA DUO

MAKE IT REAL

If the Maya-style number system is based on 20, what is the Western style based on? Yes, 10 is correct. In English, we use the prefix *deci* to mean "one-tenth" and *deca* to mean "ten." What words can you think of that use these prefixes? Decimeter (1/10 of a meter)? Decade (a period of 10 years)? Decathlon (a sports contest of 10 different events)?

What else comes in ten or tenths? Use the *deci-* or *deca-* prefix to make up names that will come in handy for what you find. After you cut a large pizza into 10 pieces, you might call out, "Come and get it! The deci-pizza is ready." If you need your brother to buy you 10 pencils in a package, you might say, "Yo! Bro! Would you mind stopping at the store to buy me a deca-pack of pencils?" And, if a scoop of ice cream costs 10 cents, you might order (dare we write it?) … a double-deca!

FIBONACCI'S NEW NUMBERS

FAST-FORWARD

In about A.D. 1200, Leonardo Fibonacci introduced the digits we use today (1, 2, 3, 4, 5, 6, 7, 8, 9, and 0) to the people of Europe. Although they were new to Europe, these symbols for numbers were nothing new to the Indian and Arab peoples of that time. This "new" system was called the *Hindu-Arabic system*, named after the people who used it first. Fibonacci had learned about it during his childhood when he lived in northern Africa with his father, who was a customs official there. Fibonacci explained this new system in a book: "There are nine figures of the Indians, 1 2 3 4 5 6 7 8 9. With these nine figures and the symbol 0, which in Arabic is called *zephirum*, any number can be written."

Unfortunately, many people didn't want to try this new method of counting. They preferred using their old system of Roman numerals, even though it was harder and more complicated to use. Finally, though, by about A.D. 1600, nearly everyone was using the Hindu-Arabic numerals.

Zero: From Zilch to Value

Although zero didn't catch on quickly even after people had been introduced to it, it did eventually gain use, first as a placeholder, and then as a number with its own value. If you can figure out why zero didn't catch on more quickly in math, you might be very close to solving the secret about math's long life.

Part III

Faster Figuring:

Knowing More—Sooner!

The Keys to the Mystery of Math

You have to be clever enough to know a clue when you are staring it in the face, so to speak!

You need to tease clues out of hiding, uncovering them from thousands of years of dirt and dust.

"What's the rush? Slow down and smell the flowers. Why is everyone in such a hurry to finish one thing so they can rush off and do another?"

Sooner or later, we can practically guarantee that you will feel that way, if you haven't already. It seems we humans are always in a hurry to accomplish more, faster.

It's a chicken-and-egg thing

Interestingly, we can learn a lot about ourselves just from what we have observed about math's long life. And if we are correct in linking the development of math with the life of individuals, it is clear that finding answers fast, then faster, then fastest is a key not only in the life of math, but in our lives, too. On closer inspection, we are faced with a *conundrum*, or puzzle: Did math drive people's lives, or did humans drive math's long life? After all, math has been here through it all, while people and their civilizations have come and gone.

According to Plato, many would say that it is necessity that drives people to invent things. And we humans sure are resourceful. But there are those who believe that often an idea catches on and before we realize it, we have changed how we do things. In no time at all, we have forgotten why we made the changes in the first place or whether they improved on anything.

As long ago as 1000 B.C., counting boards were used in China. To do what? Why, to speed up math processes! If we people were already in such a hurry more than 3,000 years ago, maybe it *is* fair to say that math was invented to help people move ahead faster and faster. After all, we haven't slowed up yet!

You need to look at some things one way and then turn them around and look at the same things another way.

You'll need to give the "handy five"—your five senses—a tough workout, because clues don't just sit around waiting to be found.

Keep that sleuthing cap on

Remember when you asked how you would know what was important? (See page 14.) Well, now that you have so many thoughts and impressions rolling around in your head, it's time for a last reminder of what it takes to be a good sleuth (see the keys on these pages).

You need to question, put forth new ideas, and listen to what others are saying.

As we near the end of our adventure, those clues will be flying by fast. Even so, take the time to have a lot of fun on this last leg of your journey, because algorithms and the high-tech abacus are definitely a good time. So, smell those flowers, while keeping your eye on the prize!

Be an Algorithm Detective

Using numbers to solve problems

How would you teach someone to tie her shoes? What is the recipe for preparing cinnamon toast? And, more to the point, what does math have to do with either of these processes? Good question. Many of us tend to think of math as times tables, figuring out problems for home-

work, and generally as something that is taught in school but is not particularly useful anyplace else. But, if that were all there is to math, why would it still be around after 35,000 years?

Despite the fact that on some days numbers might seem as if they were designed to keep you up

2000 B.C.   1500 B.C.   1000 B.C.   500 B.C.

Lots of things that we aren't familiar with are easier to do when we have a series of smaller steps to follow. That's math at work inside and outside of schools and businesses!

too late doing your homework, this is not their real purpose! Believe it or not, the process of using step-by-step instructions to complete a task, such as tying a special knot, is math at work. The instructions are called an *algorithm* (AL-geh-ri-thim). The recipe for cinnamon toast—take a piece of bread, pop it in the toaster, and when ready, spread it with butter, sugar, and cinnamon—is an algorithm, too. Lots of things that we aren't familiar with are easier to do when we have a series of smaller steps to follow. That's math at work inside and outside of schools and businesses!

TRY THIS!

An Algorithm a Day Keeps Confusion Away

It really is true that algorithms keep our levels of confusion and frustration much lower. Chances are you use a lot more than one algorithm each day, which means—surprise!—you use math many times a day. Just out of curiosity, jot down all of the math, including algorithms, that you use in one whole day. If you learn a new game, for instance, the rules of the game that tell you how to play are an algorithm. What other step-by-step algorithms can you think of? In how many ways have numbers sneaked into your life?

0	A.D. 500	A.D. 800	A.D. 1000	A.D. 1500	A.D. 1945
		Middle East: Al-Khwarizmi writes books on algorithms.		(North America) United States: George Polya publishes book on problem-solving.	

SWISH! IT'S GONE!

FAST-FORWARD

In about A.D. 800 in the Middle East, individuals were using tables covered in dust or sand to work out math problems. Similar to a chalkboard, a problem would be worked out step-by-step with the beginning parts erased as more space was needed. (Uh-oh. What do you think happened when somebody sneezed! Gezundheit!)

AN ALGORITHM MISTAKE!

Because *algorithm* is a rather difficult-sounding word, many people think it involves some type of complex mathematical process. Not so, most of the time! The word is actually the result of a mistake. A brilliant man by the name of Muhammad Bin Musa Al-Khwarizmi spent most of his life working things out on a "dust table" at his home in the Middle East. But Al-Khwarizmi's name, after it was translated from Arabic into Latin, was misread and mispronounced as "algorithm." So not only is the name misleading as to how difficult algorithms tend to be, but the word itself is just plain incorrect, too!

Lots of things that we aren't familiar with are easier to do when we have a series of smaller steps to follow.

THINK QUICK!

Lattice and algorithms

Why is the lattice multiplication method an algorithm?

Answer to the question is up the side of this page.

Make a Lattice Multiplication Puzzle

TRY THIS!

*O*ne useful algorithm that was developed in the Middle East and then later introduced to Europe by Leonardo Fibonacci is called the *lattice method of multiplication.* The grid you'll make looks like a lattice pattern. For fun, try making your own lattice puzzle.

3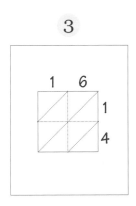

4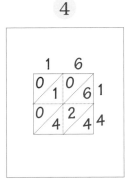

5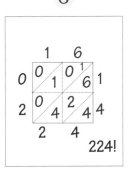

6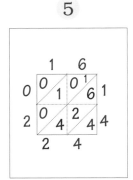

224!

You will need:
❖ Square sticky note
❖ Paper, 1 sheet
❖ Pencil
❖ Scissors

What you do:

1 Fold the square diagonally. Then flatten the paper. Refold it twice into quarters. Unfold the paper.

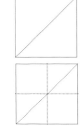

2 Make two more folds by turning in the top left and bottom right couners so that each quarter of the paper is divided into two triangles. Trace over the diagonal folds.

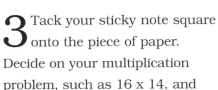

3 Tack your sticky note square onto the piece of paper. Decide on your multiplication problem, such as 16 x 14, and set up your work as shown.

4 Work with each of the four main squares separately. Multiply the aligning numbers and record the answer placing the tens in the top triangle (put 0 if there are none) and the ones in the bottom triangle. (See the example of 1 x 1 in red.)

5 Add the *diagonals*, carrying when needed. (In the example 6 + 2 + 4 = 12, you carry the 1 to the next diagonal.)

6 The answer is revealed! Read it counter-clockwise on the larger paper.

JUST FOR FUN! Draw a picture on the back of the lattice paper. It is helpful if it is of big things, like a cat, a tree, or the sun.

Cut each section apart. Challenge a friend to figure out the original number sentence. (Need help? Have her put the picture together.)

PROBLEM-SOLVING MADE OH-SO-EASY (FINALLY!)

FAST-FORWARD

"The first rule of discovery is to have brains and good luck. The second rule of discovery is to sit tight and wait until you get a bright idea."

George Polya, the mathematician who said that, moved to the United States from Europe in 1940. One of his bright ideas was to come up with a neat four-step algorithm for solving problems:

1. Understand the problem:
What is it that you want to find out?

2. Devise an algorithm:
Make a plan and use a strategy to figure out the answer. For example, you can use a strategy such as starting with what you know, looking for a pattern, making a list, drawing a picture, working backward, or making a guess and then checking it. You can also invent your own strategy.

3. Carry out your plan:
Carefully follow the steps in the plan.

4. Examine the solution:
Does the result make sense? Did the algorithm work?

TRY THIS!
Conduct an Algorithm Investigation
Think up your own problem-solving investigation. Use Polya's four-step plan to figure out the solution. Write down the algorithm, or the steps you will take to find the solution. Here are some ideas to get you started.

• What is the average number of pets owned by members of your class?

• Which person in your family reads the most?

• Where did I leave my overdue library book (or my baseball cap, favorite sweater, etc.)?

Or, make up your own algorithm on a topic that interests you!

Do Some Math in the Egyptian Style!

TRY THIS!

In ancient Egypt, many students learned math inside temple schools where boys (boys only, again!) worked out problems from papyrus study scrolls. These were called the *Kempt*. What algorithm would you use to solve this problem: 17 x 6? Is there another way to solve this? You bet there is! If you lived in ancient Egypt, you would multiply like an Egyptian, of course. Use the following algorithm to set up the number sentence 17 x 6 and solve it the Egyptian way!

```
  17
x  6
  42
  60
 102
```

```
 1      6
 2     12
 4     24
 8     48
16     96
```

```
✓ 1      6
  2     12
  4     24
  8     48
✓16     96
```

```
✓ 1    ✓ 6
  2     12
  4     24
  8     48
✓16   ✓ 96

         6
      + 96
       102
```

What you do:

1 You will need to make two columns of numbers on your paper. In the right-hand column, start with the 6 from your math problem. Complete the column by doubling the previous number.

2 Always start with a 1 in the left-hand column, placing it beside the first right-hand entry. Then continue to double the numbers in this column as well.

3 Stop doubling in the left when you have enough numbers to make the 17. Put a check beside the numbers that add to 17. This would be 16 and 1 for this math problem.

4 To find the product of 6 x 17, add the numbers in the right column that correspond to the checked numbers in the left. So, add 6 + 96 to get 102. The product of 17 x 6 is 102!

Want to impress your teacher? Try doing your math homework like an ancient Egyptian. Not so tricky once you get the hang of it, is it?

SOLVING OUR QUEST TO MATH'S SECRET LIFE!

BE A SECRET SUPER SLEUTH

Now that you have written an algorithm about something you know quite well, see if you can come up with a way to use an algorithm to find the answer to our quest: Why has math survived for more than 35,000 years?

How Far?

When?

How Many?

1. Understand the problem. (What it is you want to find out?): What is the secret to math's long life?

2. Devise an algorithm. Make a plan to solve the problem. You could use the strategies of making and then checking a guess by looking back in the book for clues. Or you could make the problem simpler by relating it to how *you* need math in everyday life. Is your life, like the lives of others before you, riddled with math situations and needs?

3. Carry out your plan. Think about the answers to your questions. Find the clues throughout the book and write them down. Then, make a list of how you use math every day. Imagine what it would be like if you couldn't calculate, measure, estimate, or count all day. What would happen?

4. Examine your solution. Does your solution to why numbers survived make sense? What do people think when you share your answer to the mystery?

What's this have to do with math's secret life?

That's a very good question. Do you know why? If you ask *why* something is included, then the answer should be an important clue. It should either contribute to your ideas thus far, or it should convince you that it is just included to confuse you. Which is it? Would we spend all of these pages just to confuse you? Here's a clue to what's going on here: Read the headlines above each section in this chapter—the big ones *and* the small ones. Together they give you some strong hints, but one headline in particular practically tells you the key to math's secret life. Another tells you how to set up your sleuthing algorithms, so you turn out a winner either way! Then, give this algorithm a try. You just might have the answer to our quest!

Hi-tech Math, the Low-tech Way

From bamboo rods to the abacus

Ask anyone who grew up in math classes without calculators, and they are sure to tell you that they did a lot of math in their heads and that long division and the like took them "forever" on paper. While most kids still use pencil and paper to do homework in elementary school, people in China have been using early calculators since about 1000 B.C. So, from then to within the time that your grandparents or great-grandparents may have been in school, math was still moving around secretively. What one group of peoples invented sometimes took thousands of years to cross borders.

Meet the Chinese!

Did you know that the ancient Chinese invented gunpowder, umbrellas, leather money, and handy calculating tools? If you were visiting ancient China and you were trying to figure out how much to pay for your steamed dumpling lunch, you could

2000 B.C.

1500 B.C.

1000 B.C.
(Asia) China:
Counting boards
used for calculation.

540 B.C.
(Asia) China:
Counting rods in use.

CHINA

use your *counting rod* type of calculator or, a little later in history, an *abacus* calculator made from beads and sticks. (The modern-type abacus that you may be familiar with didn't come into use until around A.D. 1200.) Then, when you *did* figure out how much to pay, you might store your cash on a string! (Yes, the Chinese invented some of the first metal coins, too. They made them with holes in the middle so they could carry around a "string of money.")

How could people in one country have invented so many things, far ahead of the rest of the world? Let's look at a map for clues.

See how huge the continent of Asia is? China takes up the better part of Asia, and it has a huge population. So it's no surprise that the Chinese invented many things. Ancient China had a population that probably equaled the rest of the world combined! Clearly, the Chinese were looking for ways to do math to keep track, record numbers, and then to calculate.

0   A.D. 500   A.D. 1200   A.D. 1500   A.D. 2000

(Asia) China:
Modern-type abacus
commonly used.

A Bamboo Calculator

More than 2,500 years ago, the Chinese had a convenient carry-around calculating system. It was a set of bamboo rods, or sticks. Some people who came from wealthy families might have had a set of rods made from ivory or jade. Whatever they were made of, these rods were a huge help in adding, subtracting, multiplying, and dividing. Sound a little like a calculator? You decide for yourself. After a little practice, see if you can do your math calculations more accurately and more quickly than with a pencil and paper.

Make Your Own Chinese

TRY THIS! You can make your own set of Chinese counting rods to see for yourself how helpful these were. Who knows? You may decide that these are more fun to use than a "plain old calculator!"

You will need:
❖ About 30 clean Popsicle, craft, or other sticks (see MAKE IT REAL, page 114)
❖ A piece of string, ribbon, or yarn
❖ Four sheets of paper taped together lengthwise (end to end) to make a place-value grid

What you do:

1 Practice making the Chinese rod numerals 1 to 9. Then practice some of the larger numbers. The rods that are placed vertically are called *tsungs* (ZONG) and the ones that are placed horizontally are called the *hengs* (HENG).

Counting Rods

2 Now that you've got the hang of the tsungs and hengs, practice making some larger numbers using the place-value grid. Place sticks in the place-value grid like this:

thousands	hundreds	tens	units

What number have you made? (Answer is on page 112.)

Why do you think the vertical rod numeral alternates with the horizontal rod numeral? That's right, the units and hundreds are set up vertically and the tens and thousands are set up horizontally.

What a clear and easy way to keep track of the units, tens, hundreds, and thousands digits!

Chinese rod numbers

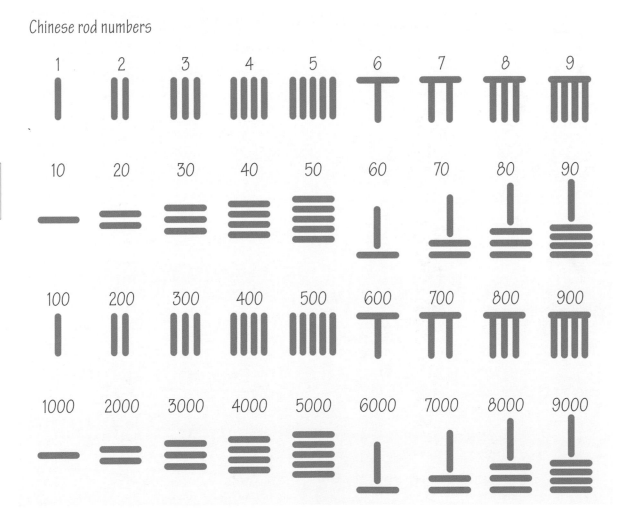

READY, SET, ADD!

Now that you are getting the "hang of the hengs," why not try adding using the rod set? It's fun! Start by setting up your rod number sentence as shown for 8 + 6:

Then, simply gather together the sticks, regrouping as necessary.

HINT: You will need to exchange two 5s in the *units* place for one 10 in the *tens* place. (Don't forget that numerals in the tens place are hengs—that is, they are placed horizontally.)

In this case, gather the four vertical rods and place them together in the units place. Next, add the two horizontal rods. They each

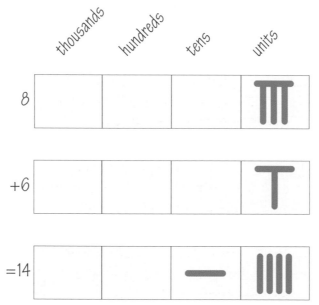

equal 5, so exchange them for one horizontal rod in the tens place.

You've done it! You have used Chinese ingenuity to work out 8 + 6! How about trying a more difficult number sentence?

For more of a challenge try something harder: How about 26 + 47?

Now, tie a ribbon or piece of yarn around your set of counting rods to keep them together until the next time you need to do some fast figuring.

WHAT'S LIGHT AND HANDY?

MAKE IT REAL

One characteristic throughout math's long life is that people did math using what was handy. At first it may have been pebbles, shells, or bones. Then people made clay counting balls with the clay that was plentiful. The quipus of long ago were made with string fashioned from the sheep's wool. It was light so that runners could traverse the empire easily and it could be carried without losing it.

The Chinese, too, wanted something that they could carry with them. Bamboo was very plentiful in ancient times and it is very light. It was the perfect choice to make rods.

When you make your calculating rods (see page 112), you can buy Popsicle or craft sticks or you can use something readily available, free, and—as with the other cultures—preferably something that is lightweight. What would you use for your calculating rod invention if you were living where you do right now, only in ancient times?

Almost Magical: The Abacus!

Did you ever have a toy abacus when you were a little kid? Lots of people had them when they were toddlers, yet traditionally they were used as calculating devices by adults. You see, around A.D. 1200, another kind of math tool was popular, also in China. The *suan pan,* the Chinese *abacus,* is still popular nowadays. (There we go again—math inventions traveling over distant miles and distant times all the way to today.) In fact, some people still prefer to use the abacus instead of using a modern electronic calculator. Those may be the same people who say that technology doesn't always help us. Can you think of a time when it was easier to do something by hand, rather than by using a machine? Hmmm.

One of many?

If you were to hold an international abacus convention, who should come? The participants from Greece, Rome, China, Japan, Russia, and other places would definitely be your honored guests. That's because China wasn't the only place to develop and use an abacus as a math tool!

Here are examples of the Chinese *suan pan,* the Japanese *soroban* (sore-oh-ban), and the Russian *schoty* (SHAW-tee).

Can you see the differences between the Chinese abacus and the others? Which of these do you think would be the easiest to use?

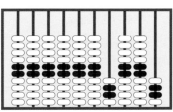

Russian schoty (SHAW-tee)

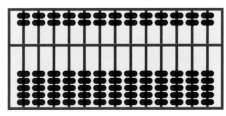

Chinese suan pan

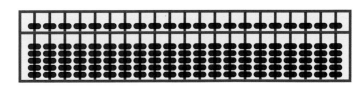

Japanese soroban (sore-oh-ban)

Make Your Own Chinese Abacus

TRY THIS!

Whether you decide this is the ultimate early invention or you are doing just fine with that handy little inexpensive calculator in your backpack, you'll want to make one of these and give it a try. It is amazing to think that this was invented so long ago. It's hard to believe. Just think, you are using a piece of early history!

You will need:

❖ Ruler

❖ Pen and pencil

❖ A shoe-box lid

❖ Wire (We like the plastic-coated kind from the hardware store.)

❖ 8 "heaven" beads of one color

❖ 20 "earth" beads of another color

❖ 1 dowel slightly wider than the box for a dividing rod

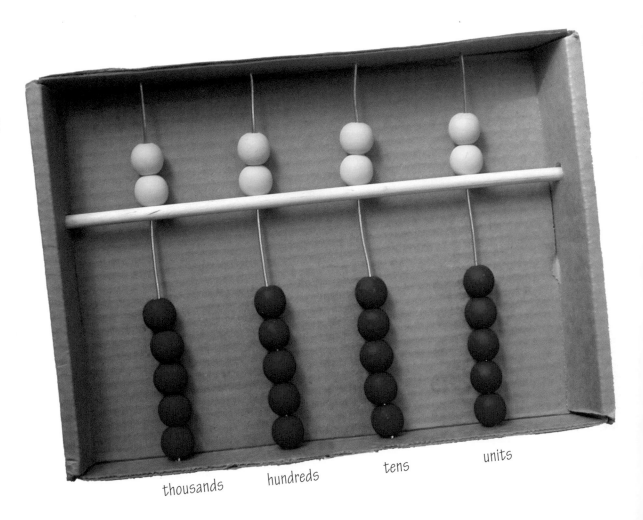

thousands   hundreds   tens   units

What you do:

1 Make marks across the lower side of the box where the holes for the wire rods will go. Use a ruler and a pencil to make four evenly spaced marks far enough away from the back so that the beads can move. Mark the upper side in the same way.

2 Have an adult help you use a pen point to poke a hole through each of the marks you made.

3 Cut four wires about 2" (5 cm) longer than the box. Push the wire through the holes and bend each end so that the wire doesn't fall out.

4 Place five earth beads of one color and two heaven beads of another color onto the wire as shown.

5 Put three more wires into place and add the heaven and earth beads.

6 Make a mark on the left and right sides of the box for the dividing rod. Place the marks about one-third of the way from the top, make sure they are even. Pake a hole through each of the marks. Push the heaven beads up and the earth beads down. Then push the dowel through to make a dividing rod.

7 Starting from the right, label the wires: units, tens, hundreds, and thousands. Now you can learn to form numbers. (See page 118.)

thousands hundreds tens units

Because we know how you like added challenges (right?), you can use the abacus to practice decimal numbers if you label the right-hand wire hundredths, the second wire tenths, the third wire units, and the left-hand wire tens.

Moving Heaven and Earth on the Abacus!

TRY THIS!

It's fun to practice forming numbers on the abacus! You'll need to move heaven and earth (beads, that is) to form these numbers, though! Just like in our modern number system, each beaded string is a place value, starting at the right with the units place. On each string, the (top) heaven beads are each worth five units and the (bottom) earth beads

Just think, you are using a piece of early history!

are each worth one unit. (Psst! Heaven = above or top; earth = below or bottom. But you were already using that mnemonic device, weren't you?)

After you learn to make these, try a few others until you feel comfortable.

How about making the number for the year you were born? Aha, right, got it?

(If not, not to worry; just go back to some double-digit numbers until you feel more comfortable with it.)

1. Get ready by pushing all the beads away from the center.

thousands hundreds tens units

2. Make the number 7 like this:

3. Now, try making 37. Your abacus should look like this:

TAKE THE ABACUS CHALLENGE

MAKE IT REAL

In 1945, a calculating race was held using a Japanese soroban that cost about 25 cents against a United States Army adding machine that cost $700. The outcome surprised many people! Kiyoshi Matsuzaki, nicknamed

"The Hands," used a soroban to win the contest against Thomas Ian Deering on an electric adding machine. With fewer mistakes and time to spare, the soroban won hands down!

Are you ready to take the abacus challenge—you on the abacus versus someone else on a calculator?

1. Ask someone to be a referee. For a warm-up, the referee has a stopwatch and two dice to generate the numbers.

2. At the count of three, the referee starts the stopwatch and then rolls the dice. Race against your calculator opponent to be the first one to show the

sum of the two dice on your Chinese abacus.

3. Now, try something more challenging, like a number sentence.

The referee randomly calls out two larger numbers to add. Race your opponent again. Who was able to show the answer first?

The Abacus Appeal

So, what do you think? Is an abacus more fun and more efficient than the math tools you use today? Do you feel as if you are really involved in the process because you are moving the beads and thinking fast? Those are interesting issues, because a lot of inventive thinking comes about when you are "into," or involved in, something. Is the calculator too separate from you and your thought process?

What is really of interest with regard to our search for the secret to the long life of math and numbers is that while a quick and accurate calculaing device (the abacus) was invented in one part of the world, Roman numerals that were very awkward to calculate with were in use in another part of the world. Assuming all peoples are equally capable of invention, what is the difference? Answer that and you will have solved the mystery!

Solve the Mystery of Math's Longevity

Find the "common denominator" across the ages (& pages)

Well, we're at a good stopping place for now. Of course, there is so much more to math's mysterious ability to sustain itself (or to be sustained by us). Times were definitely changing at this point in math's life, and independent civilizations were becoming aware of one another's existence. Ideas were being carried across the oceans, first in the simplest of ways as ships began to bring food and spices as well as observations about others from one continent to another, and then in more immediate ways. Today, it seems as if ideas travel almost as fast as we can think of them!

Understanding the secret to math's role in global culture and its longevity is no longer a matter of searching through ancient

> "Could it be that no matter who our ancestors are, when or where they lived, or what color their skin was, we humans are all very much alike?"
>
> —Anonymous

cultures to unearth artifacts as we try to reconstruct how math has shaped us or how we have shaped it.

Yet, the "common denominator" remains very much the same today as it was back then. (We use the math term "common denominator" in the sense that these are shared attributes, or themes, that kept numbers and math alive.) The most important of those common denominators embodies the mysterious secret to math's long, long life.

The Secret Super Sleuth reveals the secret to math's life

You don't really need us anymore. Truthfully, you already know the answer to math's secret life, even if you don't feel as if you do—yet.

You can give your detective summation now if you like, or you can use these last clues. We're proud of you for all you've accomplished and for being such an amazing detective. We hope you've had fun, too, and that what you've learned about math, about human nature and people the world over, and about yourself will stay with you a long time.

So here we go—the last clues!

The last clues!

Clue #1
Blurt it out—right off the top of your head!

That's right. Spontaneity is a great thing. Don't think about it too much, just say it! Or, brainstorm with some others.

• Jot down the ideas or answers that interest or amuse you—and especially the ones that take you totally by surprise.

Clue #2
Why, oh why, did math grow here?

Have you noticed how much we have learned about human nature (that is how human beings seem to react, behave, and live their lives) by looking at how math has "lived" its life? In a way, you might say that math reveals character-istics about people that repeat themselves from one civilization to another.

• Look at the different cultures we visited and ask yourself "why" math and numbers took root there.

Clue #3
One-word impressions

Flip through the pages and jot down *single words* about the different kinds of keeping track and how and why they were used. Why tally sticks? Why counting balls? Why quipus?

• Look over your words and see if a theme develops. That will be a big clue as to how math survived and why.

Clue #4
People! People! People!

You've met people who lived in the far corners of the earth, thinking they were the only humans. You've met people who developed complex civilizations from scratch. You've met people who made hatch marks 35,000 years ago and people who used double tallies in England as recently as 200 years ago.

• What conclusions have you drawn about people the world over throughout all time? What does this have to do with the secret to math's longevity?

Clue #5
Across great distances?

Ask yourself (and then answer yourself): Could math have traveled "on its own" from here to there?

• Explain how math traveled great distances without a lot of human communication.

Clue #6
Throughout thousands upon thousands of years?

Think about the enormous time spans separating similar math concepts. How is it that some "math inventions" were so similar?

• Explain how math traveled back and forth in time without human communication or even human contact with artifacts. How is it that so many similar ideas came about even when separated by time and distance?

Clue #7
Try 'em on!

You know how it is when you are trying on a new pair of jeans in the store. Maybe a friend keeps telling you that each pair looks fine, but you keep trying different ones. And then, you put on a pair and you don't even ask how it looks on you. You just know this is the pair because it feels right. Well, that is what we all need to do right now. That is, we need to try on different ideas to find the key to math's long and secret life.

• You'll know when you find the answer, just as you know when you find the perfect pair of jeans. It will feel just right!

Index

F

Fibonacci, Leonardo (Italian mathematician), 91, 96, 105
finger counting, 30–35, 80
fractions, 86–88

G

Glyphs. *See* hieroglyphics
Greece, 33, 115

H

hatch marks, 16–22, 50. *See also* tallies
hieroglyphics (glyphs), 78–88
Hindu-Arabic number system, 96
Horus, Eye of, 86–88
Hypatia of Alexandria (early mathematician), 7

I

importance of math, 6–7
Incan quipus and quipucamayocs, 37, 39–46
India, 91, 92

J

Japan
    knots, 39, 42
    soroban (abacus), 115, 118

K

ketsujo, 42. *See also* Japan: knots
Al-Khwarizmi (Arabic mathematician), 103, 104

knots, 37–46

L

lattice multiplication grid, 104–105
loans and double tally sticks, 23–27

M

math sleuth, being, 7–9, 14–15, 51, 55, 58–59, 64, 74, 89, 100–101, 108–109, 120–123
Mayan number system, 82, 91, 92–95
measurement, 36
Mesopotamia, 40, 61, 63, 65, 112. *See also* Babylon
Middle East. *See also* Babylon; Mesopotamia
    clay tokens, 60–68
    empty place value, 90
    knots, 39
    written numerals, 61, 71
mnemonic devices, 114
Morra, 33
multiplication, 53, 104–105. *See also* computation

N

Native Americans. *See* American Indians
nature count, American Indian-style, 20–21
numerals. *See* written number systems

O

obsolescence, 68
origins of math. *See also* math sleuth, being

algorithms, 102–104
diverse origins, 15, 49, 70–71
finger counting, 30–32
hatch marks, 16–17
Hindu-Arabic number system, 96
place value, 92
Roman numerals, 49–51, 55
universality of math, 58, 71
written number systems, 59–68

P

paper, 82
papier-mâché recipe, 67
Papua New Guinea, 31
papyrus, 83. *See also* Egypt, ancient
pebbles, 40, 60–62
Persia, ancient, 42
place value
    abacus, 116–118
    Chinese tsung-heng system, 113–114
    cuneiform awkward, 73, 92
    empty place value, 90, 92 (*See also* zero)
    origins, 92
    quipus and other knotted tallies, 37, 43–45
Plato (Greek philosopher), 101
Polya, George, 103, 106
positive and negative numbers, 46
problem-solving. *See* algorithms; computation

Q

quipus and quipucamayocs, 37–46, 92, 112

Index

Resources

RESOURCES FOR READERS

The Adventures of Penrose the Mathematical Cat by Theoni Pappas (Wide World Publishing, 1997)

Ask Dr. Math (website) <http://mathforum.org/dr.math/>

From Zero to Ten: The Story of Numbers by Vivian French and Ross Collins (Oxford University Press, 2000)

The History of Counting by Denise Schmandt-Besserat (Morrow Junior Books, 1999)

How to Count Like a Martian by Glory St. John (Random House Children's Books, 1975)

The MacTutor History of Mathematics Archive (website) <http://www-history.mcs.st-andrews.ac.uk/history/index.html>

Moja Means One: Swahili Counting Book by Muriel L. Feelings (Dial Books for Young Readers, 1971)

REFERENCES

Ascher, Marcia. *Ethnomathematics: A Multicultural View of Mathematical Ideas.* Belmont, CA: Wadsworth, Inc., 1991.

Ascher, Marcia. *Mathematics Elsewhere: An Exploration of Ideas Across Cultures.* Princeton, NJ: Princeton University Press, 2002.

Ascher, Marcia. *Mathematics of the Incas: Code of the Quipu.* New York: Dover Publications, 1997.

Closs, Michael P., ed. *Native American Mathematics.* Austin, TX: University of Texas Press, 1986.

Gerdes, Paulus, ed. *Geometry from Africa: Mathematical and Educational Explorations.* The Mathematical Association of America, 1999.

Gillings, Richard J. *Mathematics in the Time of the Pharoahs.* Cambridge, MA: MIT Press, 1972.

Ifrah, Georges. *The Universal History of Numbers: From Prehistory to the Invention of the Computer.* New York: John Wiley & Sons, Inc., 2000.

Joseph, George Gheverghese. *The Crest of the Peacock: Non-European Roots of Mathematics.* Princeton, NJ: Princeton University Press, 2000.

Katz, Victor J. *A History of Mathematics: An Introduction.* New York: HarperCollins, 1993.

Zaslavsky, Claudia. *Africa Counts: Number and Pattern in African Culture.* Chicago: Lawrence Hill Books (an imprint of Chicago Review Press), 1999.

Zaslavsky, Claudia. *Math Games and Activities from Around the World.* Chicago: Chicago Review Press, 1998.

More Good Books from Williamson

The following Williamson Kids Can! ® Books are for ages 7 to 14 are each 128 to 160 pages, fully illustrated, trade paper, 11 x 8 1/2, $12.95 U.S. (Prices may be higher in Canada.) To order, please see below.

Real-World Math for Hands-On Fun!
by Cindy A. Littlefield

Parents' Choice Recommended
The Kids' Book of Weather Forecasting
Build a Weather Station, "Read" the Sky & Make Predictions!
with meteorologist Mark Breen & Kathleen Friestad

Parents' Choice Silver Honor Award
Awesome OCEAN SCIENCE!
Investigating the Secrets of the Underwater World
by Cindy A. Littlefield

Benjamin Franklin Best Juvenile Nonfiction Award
Learning® Magazine Teachers' Choice Award
Super Science Concoctions
50 Mysterious Mixtures for Fabulous Fun
by Jill Frankel Hauser

Parents' Choice Silver Honor Award
Fizz, Bubble & Flash!
Element Explorations & Atom Adventures for Hands-On Science Fun!
by Anita Brandolini, Ph.D.

Parents' Choice Recommended
Children's Digest Health Education Award
The Kids' Guide to FIRST AID
All about Bruises, Burns, Stings, Sprains & Other Ouches
by Karen Buhler Gale, R.N.

Parents' Choice Gold Award
Dr. Toy Best Vacation Product
The Kids' Nature Book
365 Indoor/Outdoor Activities & Experiences
by Susan Milord

Using Color in Your Art!
Choosing Colors for Impact & Pizzazz
by Sandi Henry, full-color

Parents' Choice Gold Award
Oppenheim Toy Portfolio Best Book Award
The Kids' Multicultural Art Book
Art & Craft Experiences from Around the World
by Alexandra M. Terzian

Selection of Book-of-the-Month; Scholastic Book Clubs
Kids Cook!
Fabulous Food for the Whole Family
by Sarah Williamson and Zachary Williamson

Parents' Choice Approved
Great Games!
Old & New, Indoor/Outdoor, Travel, Board, Ball & Word
by Sam Taggar

Kids Write!
Fantasy & Sci Fi, Mystery, Autobiography, Adventure & More!
Rebecca Olien

Parents' Choice Gold Award
Benjamin Franklin Best Juvenile Nonfiction Award
Kids Make Music!
Clapping and Tapping from Bach to Rock
by Avery Hart and Paul Mantell

WordPlay Café
Cool Codes, Priceless Punzles ® & Phantastic Phonetic Phun
by Michael Kline

Parents' Choice Recommended
Kids' Easy-to-Create Wildlife Habitats
for small spaces in the city, suburbs & countryside
by Emily Stetson

Oppenheim Toy Portfolio Best Book Award
Parents' Choice Approved
Summer Fun!
60 Activities for a Kid-Perfect Summer
by Susan Williamson

American Institute of Physics Science Writing Award
Parents' Choice Honor Award
Gizmos & Gadgets
Creating Science Contraptions that Work (& Knowing Why)
by Jill Frankel Hauser

In the Days of Dinosaurs
A Rhyming Romp through Dino History
by Howard Temperley
64 pages, 8 1/2 x 11, full-color, $9.95

Visit Our Website!
www.williamsonbooks.com
or www.Idealsbooks.com